John G. O. Miranda

S0-EBR-268

DISCARD

Short-Term Financial Management
How to Improve Financial Results—Now!

Also by Frank C. Wilson
Industrial Cost Controls

Short-Term Financial Management

How to Improve Financial Results—Now!

FRANK C. WILSON

1975

Dow Jones-Irwin, Inc.   Homewood, Illinois   60430

© DOW JONES-IRWIN, INC., 1975

All rights reserved. No part of this publication may be
reproduced, stored in a retrieval system, or transmitted,
in any form or by any means, electronic, mechanical,
photocopying, recording, or otherwise, without the prior
written permission of the publisher.

This publication is designed to provide accurate and
authoritative information in regard to the subject matter
covered. It is sold with the understanding that the
publisher is not engaged in rendering legal, accounting, or
other professional service. If legal advice or other expert
assistance is required, the services of a competent
professional person should be sought.
*From a Declaration of Principles jointly adopted by a Committee
of the American Bar Association and a Committee of Publishers.*

First Printing, October 1975

ISBN 0-87094-106-2
Library of Congress Catalog Card No. 75–27605
Printed in the United States of America

*This book is dedicated to my wife, Anne,
who was a constant source of help, inspiration,
and encouragement.*

*To my secretary, Betty B. Lathem,
who never lost patience with my many drafts
and corrections and without whose help,
this writing would never have been
completed.*

*To W. B. Coffey, Controller, and his staff
at WestPoint Pepperell, Dalton, Georgia,
who verified the mathematics.*

FEB 1 1985

Preface

Short-Term Financial Management is written to help managers increase profits in a complex business environment and to assist them in mastering events as they occur.

This book is a systematic approach to increasing profits in the short term—the next 12 to 18 months. It provides management with tested methods that will significantly improve decision making and problem solving ability—today!

Short-Term Financial Management is addressed to the following questions.

1. How can we operate in the situation which exists now?
2. What can be done in each area of the business—marketing, data processing, product planning, manufacturing efficiencies, inventory control, customer service, and communications—to increase effectiveness and reduce costs *now*?

Success or the appearance of success on the Profit and Loss statement can be misleading. Higher sales and good profit increases can camouflage problems and fail to point up the importance of cash flow to sustain growth in inflationary times. Inventory profits can mask real problems. These unreal financial improvements can cause managers to make serious strategic mistakes. They can cause managers to miss excellent opportunities to improve results in the business.

I have described short-term financial management techniques which will improve results immediately to survive a present crisis and build a sounder foundation for growth in the years ahead.

Too often, we look too far into the future. Long-range planning is important, but for most of us the real need is to get results now or there may not be a business in the long term. This book focuses on short-term actions to avoid a crisis or turn a business in trouble around while not overlooking medium- and long-range possibilities.

I do not apologize for some of the firm statements made in this book about certain principles of business management. There are some absolutes in the world of business that are sound and valid. For these, there is no need for compromise, indifference, or indecision.

Good business results do not occur by chance. They must be planned and managed on a systematic basis.

Gainesville, Georgia
September 1975

FRANK C. WILSON, P. E., (CMC)

Acknowledgments

Consulting Editors

John Dixon
Division President
Sikes Corporation
Lakeland, Florida

Morton Broffman
Director
Exchange National Bank of Chicago
Chicago, Illinois

Reading Editors

Klaus Holler
Director
Dura Tufting GMBH
Fulda, West Germany

Enrique Loppacher
Deputy Manager
Forbo Betriebs AG
Zurich, Switzerland

Susumu Ohara
Editor
Japan Economic Journal
Otemachi Chiyoda-ku
Tokyo, Japan

Myles Hartley
Director
Shaw Carpets Limited
Darton, Barnsley, Yorkshire, England

Consulting editors and reading editors have added to the breadth, accuracy, and scope of this book. The participation as a consulting or reading editor does not imply that each concurs with every concept or detail of this book. They are not responsible for any errors or omissions. Full responsibility rests with the author.

Author's Note

The following books provide supplementary reading for managers at all levels. Management education—either academic or personal—is not complete unless these books have been studied. These texts are references for this publication.

Priority One

Sloan, Alfred P., Jr. *My Years With General Motors.* Garden City, N.Y.: Doubleday & Co., Inc., 1963.

Drucker, Peter F. *Managing For Results.* New York: Harper & Row, Publishers, 1964.

Levitt, Theodore. *Innovations In Marketing.* New York: McGraw-Hill Book Company, 1962.

Priority Two

Shuman, James B. *The Kondratieff Wave.* New York: World Publishing, 1972.

Wilson, Frank C. *Industrial Cost Controls.* 2d printing. Englewood Cliffs, N.J.: Prentice-Hall, Inc., 1973.

Daughen, Joseph R., and Binzen, Peter. *The Wreck of the Penn Central.* Boston: Little, Brown and Company, 1971.

Contents

Systematic Cost Reduction. Corporate Office Expenses. Data Processing Expenses. Company versus Commercial Aircraft. Company Trucks. Company Cars. Executive Privileges. Telephone Service. Advertising and Sales Promotion. Other Expense Reductions. Coping with the Business Slowdown: *A Case Study*. *Maintaining Sales*. *Cost Reduction*. *Stretching Out Capital Expenditures*. Recommendations to Improve Short-Term Financial Management.

section four

Acquisition Analysis: *Planning Acquisition Strategy.* *Finding Acquisition Candidates. Financial Projection. Tax Implications. Terms of Acquisition. Integrating the Acquisition into the Organization. Deterioration of Existing Operations.* Spin-Off of an Operation: *Case Study. Investment and Profit Analysis. Cash Employed Analysis. Cash Flow Analysis.* Recommendations to Improve Short-Term Financial Management.

Cash Strategy. Financial Structure. Cash Forecasting. Short-Term Cash Management. Cash Efficiency. Factoring. Leasing. Interest Burden. Recommendations to Improve Short-Term Financial Management.

section one

Planned Systematic Management
Turnaround Management
Product Explosion

chapter ONE

Planned Systematic Management

Determine where you are going, start in that direction, and keep on going.

Keys to Professional Management

Pooh Bear was in the forest one day and walked around a tree. He observed a certain set of tracks and said to himself, "There may be a Woozle in the forest. I must find him." So he followed the tracks around the tree again only to find two sets of tracks. "It's a very funny thing," said Bear, "But there seems to be two animals now." Continuing to follow the tracks, Pooh suddenly stopped, "A third animal has joined the other two!"

Pooh Bear then sat down on a log, scratched his head, and said, "I have been Foolish & Deluded. I am a Bear of No Brain at All."[1]

Sometimes, managers also go around in circles, following the wrong tracks and misreading important signals. They solve the same problems year after year. Managers should understand the factors which have an impact both in the short term and in the long term of their business.

Even success can be a problem. Success can mask potentially dangerous situations and cause managers to miss opportunities in their particular sphere of activities. Success can allow dangerous situations to be created. Systematic management is a way to identify problems and their symptoms which, if acted on in the short term, will prevent tomorrow's problems.

In the case where a business is in trouble or experiences a crisis which threatens its very existence, short-term decisions and actions may be required. These may be expendable in a short term or reversible in the long term, simply to enable survival in the short term and viability in the medium- or long-term perspective.

Business and industry are in a new era of social, economic, and political influence. A new age of competitiveness exists. Improving the return on capital employed through improved efficiency and innovative action in marketing, in manufacturing, and in other functions will require a sharpening of the basic skills and understanding of business. Systematic management can help to meet the new challenge through short-term financial planning.

Throughout business history, examples of cyclical performance are found

---

[1] A. A. Milne, *The World of Pooh* (New York: E. P. Dutton & Company, Inc., 1957), pp. 36–44.

5

in most industries. There is a rise to higher sales and profits; then, a leveling and decline. A crisis frequently follows which focuses management's attention on the need for decisions and actions to allow the enterprise to rebuild performance. These crises which are brought about by lower sales, change in technology, decline in efficiency, and poor profit performance need not happen.

Crises can be avoided by managers recognizing the stage of this cycle in their business. By anticipating the next stage, managers can make decisions and take corrective actions to maintain control of the business and avoid this cyclical performance. Otherwise, managers will find their options are limited and controlled by events (lack of cash, loan repayment demands).

With a rapidly changing business environment—materials, markets, technology, and information systems—there is an urgent need for a high level of management performance. Professional management in all areas of the business enterprise is essential.

Even in the complex world of statistics, management science, and computer technology, excellent management is still the ability to do simple things well. It is applying common sense and experience to knowledge in a planned, organized manner on a day-to-day basis.

ASKING THE RIGHT QUESTIONS

A major part of a manager's job is asking the right questions.

These questions concern themselves with events that occur outside the business as well as inside the business. These questions are generally interrelated.

At first glance, some outside events may seem to have no real impact on the business. Yet, when these conditions are looked at in a broader dimension, they will be seen as important to the success of the enterprise, both in the short and long term.

As an example, how many managers have asked the questions about the effect of energy costs on their business? These increases and similar changes will be of considerable consequence to nearly every business, now and in the future.

Asking the right questions is more important than coming up with vital answers to the wrong questions.

There are three types of questions:

1. False, or the wrong questions.
2. True, but trivial questions.
3. True, well defined, and important questions.

The key is to avoid the wrong questions and separate the true and important questions from those which are trivial. Once a question is defined and found valid, then managers must concentrate on those few areas where results will be exceptional. In the short term, it may be raw material cost. In another case, it may be physical distribution (an often neglected area), or it may be pricing the product mix. All of these are critical areas in most businesses and require a major part of management's time.

Efficiency should not be confused with managerial effectiveness. Effectiveness has been defined as determining what should be done and doing it; whereas efficiency can be doing a good job at work of no consequence. Thus, when managers and employees spend long hours and do hard work in unnecessary areas, their performance is neither efficient nor effective.

The 80–20 principle seems to work worldwide. Generally, 15 to 25 percent of our items contribute significantly to profits. The remaining 75 to 85 percent inflate costs and have very little impact on results.

This is not to imply that all the activities in the 75 to 85 percent category should be discontinued. For products, many stockkeeping items are required to balance a product line or provide the range of items to fill customer needs —sizes, colors, or price points. Certainly, these should be evaluated before action is taken to discontinue or scale down these items in the product program.

People (our resource with the most potential) spend most of their time on transactions—orders, invoices, stockkeeping items, and other factors associated with complexity. Frequently, personnel devote the majority of their time to true and trivial problems, rather than to those which will contribute useful, constructive, and lasting results.

There should be no such function as staff personnel or staff operations. Every person, every activity, and every expense should be productive, or it should be eliminated. Large computer installations, excessive corporate offices, and expenses to satisfy the ego of executives—company aircraft, high travel expenses, and prestigious cars—are excellent opportunities for cost reduction to improve short-term financial results.

The return on investment or expenditure justification for a computer installation should be identical to that for production equipment. Both are required to produce and service a product. Otherwise, the funds should not be expended. Electronic data processing and other similar functions should be appraised using the same criteria as manufacturing operations, marketing efficiency, or distribution costs.

Many students of business believe that successful management is a mystic intuition given to only a few. Nothing could be further from the truth!

To be a professional in the truest sense, the manager's performance will not just be satisfactory—it will be outstanding!

What are the characteristics of those outstanding managers, those few men and women who achieve superior results on a continuing basis?

First, what are some characteristics that may not be common among these few managers? Some seldom exercise and are overweight; others are specimens of physical health. Many approach their decisions in an agonizing way; others

**CHARACTER-
ISTICS OF
OUTSTANDING
MANAGERS**

make decisions and walk away from them relatively unconcerned, at least outwardly. Some have strong academic backgrounds; others come up through the ranks with little formal academic training.

 There are factors which are distinctive among the truly good managers. These executives:

1. Understand that their job is to get economic results now, and to make the resources within their jurisdiction profitable.
2. Plan ahead—either in a formal manner or in their own way—while concentrating on operations today.
3. Have an extraordinary ability to communicate and instill confidence in their people to achieve improved performance.
4. Know their business in total, not just an isolated function or part.
5. Use their time wisely.
6. Carefully consider all aspects of their decisions on an analytical and objective basis in conjunction with judgment and experience (they take calculated risks only).
7. Have an amazing ability to simplify situations, to apply common sense in conjunction with knowledge and intelligence.
8. Provide leadership—not genius—in a methodical, organized manner.
9. Maintain a calm personnel climate of security, confidence, and integrity.
10. Work with a spirit of adventure which results in creativity and innovation among the people in the business.
11. Read and learn continually; they are never content with their knowledge of management, of their business, or of their industry.
12. Are honest, and keep their people informed.
13. Listen well!

And, there are others, too!

Good managers are generally decisive. Indecision is a poison that paralyzes. Management is a never-ending series of choices and accepting the risks that go with these choices.

Good management practices are deceptively simple. Too often, they are made complex.

Good management is neither an art nor a science. It is a discipline. The practices of good management become a habit.

A leading golfer, after winning a narrow victory in a professional tournament, was confronted by a reporter who commented on his luck. He responded, "The more I practice, the luckier I get." And so it is with management, too. The more the disciplines of good management are practiced, the more managers' performances improve.

The keys to successful management are skills that can be learned. They do not come by themselves; they require practice on a continuing basis to be learned properly.

This book deals with management skills—methods that can be learned.

A management audit of the business is a good way to find those areas where performance can be improved, determine the areas of weakness which require strengthening, and obtain a perspective of the company versus competition.

Managers would not think of closing a fiscal year without an audit of their financial records. Many are accustomed to having periodic marketing audits. Management, too, can be analyzed through a management audit, either by internal or external personnel, on an objective and analytical basis. These audits ask the right questions, the true and important questions about business. This requires a commitment from key management to bring out the right questions.

Typical questions contained in a management audit of executive management are displayed in Figure 1–1. Each major division (sales, merchandising and product planning, manufacturing, distribution, administration, or others) can have a separate set of questions for each function or subfunction. These questions should be designed to find the state of the business now. Then, detailed analysis can be initiated assigning specific responsibility and target dates for correction.

Point values can be assigned based on the relative impact of the question on performance. Then, monthly or quarterly comparisons can be made (Figure 1–2) to determine which functions are improving and which may be slipping in performance. Changes in the trend of operations can be detected.

Questions for a management audit can change from year to year depending on the condition of the business, its size, and complexity. In developing the questions, each supervisor or manager can set his objectives and begin managing toward those objectives.

The questions illustrated in Figure 1–1 are conceptual, for they deal with management. Questions developed for individual departments or cost centers could be more specific as listed below.

1. Can productivity be increased by a given targeted percentage in the short term?
2. Can off-quality levels be reduced in the next six months?
3. Can the reliability of customer service be improved in the immediate future?

Of course, where specific numbers or absolute units exist, the questions should set precise targets. As an example, can the customer service level improve to the 75 percent level from the 70 percent level existing six months earlier?

When using specific targets, the questions would have to be modified as the audits move from time period to time period.

FIGURE 1–1
Management Audit

Yes	No		
___	___	1.	Have profits declined in recent months or can a decline be expected in the short term?
___	___	2.	Is, or will, cash be available to finance the business and repay current debt commitments?
___	___	3.	Does the present management have the capability or motivation to significantly improve performance in the short term?
___	___	4.	Are accounts receivable of satisfactory quality and within general industry terms?
___	___	5.	Within the accounts receivable, are there customers that are past due from whom collections can be obtained or sales discontinued?
___	___	6.	Are sales concentrated in a relatively few stockkeeping items or customers?
___	___	7.	Do existing products adequately fulfill market needs for the immediate future?
___	___	8.	Are there any new products available (or modifications to existing products) which could generate sales and earnings with expenses within the capability of present financing?
___	___	9.	Are inventories priced at a value consistent with a reasonably efficient firm in the industry?
___	___	10.	Is there a possibility of losses as a result of discontinued, obsolete, off-quality, or other nonstandard merchandise in inventories or material commitments?
___	___	11.	Can production planning be improved to reduce funds utilized in inventories—raw materials, work-in-process, and finished goods?
___	___	12.	Are there opportunities for improvement in the product mix?
___	___	13.	Does idle capacity exist in any process, plant, or other facility?
___	___	14.	Are there opportunities for cost or expense reduction in any facet of the business?
___	___	15.	Is there a potential acquisition available within the capability of the firm to improve integrated manufacturing and become more cost competitive?
___	___	16.	Is there any segment, subsidiary, division, or plant of the business which could be spun-off to quickly reduce losses or generate cash?

FIGURE 1–1 (continued)

Yes	No		
———	———	17.	Do any contracts come up for negotiation which could result in higher costs, strikes, or other disruptions to the business?
———	———	18.	Can advertising and promotion expenditures be reduced or made more effective in the next 12 to 18 months?
———	———	19.	Are there certain costs—outlying warehouses, corporate offices, division staffs, data processing facilities, trucking operations, company aircraft, or similar items —which could be reduced or eliminated in the short term, even if these must be added back in the long term?
———	———	20.	Has an analysis been made of the firm as compared to one significant competitor considering factors of sales, profits, growth, strengths, and weaknesses?
═══	═══		Totals

Note: To arrive at the total score, sum the total number of "Yes" answers and multiply by five.

FIGURE 1–2

Management Audit Control Report

		Last Year by Quarters				Current Year by Quarters			
Function or Subfunction		*1*	*2*	*3*	*4*	*1*	*2*	*3*	*4*
I.	Executive management.................	70	75	80	80	80			
II.	Sales...............................	65	70	75	75	70			
III.	Merchandising and product planning.....	57	61	67	77	85			
	Department subfunctions:								
	a. Market research.................	15	15	16	17	17			
	b. Product planning...............	10	13	15	16	17			
	c. Market planning................	12	13	12	15	15			
	d. Sales promotion.................	9	9	9	12	16			
	e. Sales administration.............	11	11	15	17	20			
IV.	Manufacturing........................	75	80	80	85	90			
V.	Distribution..........................	70	70	75	80	85			
VI.	Administration........................	55	60	70	75	80			
	Totals...........................	392	416	447	472	490	—	—	—

**RECOMMENDA-
TIONS TO
IMPROVE SHORT-
TERM FINANCIAL
MANAGEMENT**

Managers should:

Compare their management characteristics with those listed in this chapter to determine opportunities for improvement.

Request each person at the appropriate management level to develop sets of questions—questions which would be the key points to managing and controlling each area of responsibility.

Check the vital areas—financing, inventories, products, management, and costs—to find out the health of the business. Does a crisis exist or do symptoms of an approaching one exist? Within what time frame must action be taken to improve performance?

Once these questions have been developed individually, the management team can sit down together and develop the policies, the strategies, and the guidelines for the business. Then, performance against these objectives can be monitored with periodic management audits.

SUMMARY

Planned systematic management is the key to professional management at all levels. This chapter contains a checklist of keys which distinguish those few superior managers.

Management practices are deceptively simple. Good management is neither an art nor a science; it is a discipline. Practices of good management become a habit. They are skills which can be learned.

A management audit is the starting point for systematic management. It is a good way to analyze the business operations. By charting the results, managers can detect improvements or changes in trend by activity or function depending on the detail of the audit.

A management audit is an excellent way of finding out those areas of the firm where substantial improvement can be achieved. It can point out those few areas where small changes can have a major impact on improving short-term financial performance. It can aid in setting targets and managing by these objectives.

This chapter illustrates how to develop and use a management audit. The following chapters point out more specific, more detailed ways of improving financial results—organizational effectiveness, simplification of products, reduction of transactions, engineered budget control, pricing, inventory management, profit improvement, money management, and acquisition analysis.

chapter *TWO*

Turnaround Management

The first priority of management is improving performance now, surviving the present crisis or preventing disaster—or, there will be no business to manage strategically in the long term. Some decisions, in this situation, are expendable in the short term or reversible in the long term.

Surviving in the Short Term

TURNAROUND MANAGEMENT is improving results in a poorly performing business. The initial step is assessing the state of the business and its management (Chapter One, Management Audit).

Defining the expressions "poorly" or "degree of crisis" is essential. A well financed firm in trouble can take time (up to three years) to reverse the existing situation. A business in a loss situation with little cash flow must take actions quickly. In this second case, the question becomes one of surviving in the short term or there will be no long-term business.

In a booming economy, symptoms of an approaching crisis may be masked or allowed to mature by external factors.

On the down side of a business cycle, most firms do not go into a loss situation gradually. Losses and the magnitude of the crisis increase at an accelerated (even a frightening) rate. This is particularly true of the marginal company in times of change from good economic conditions to a slowdown.

The marginal company normally has poor cash flow. Consequently, in a downturn, the poorly performing business can quickly—very quickly—face bankruptcy or financial restructuring.

For the questionable divisions in a large corporate enterprise which is healthy, the result is either sell-off the business or shutdown with heavy one-time losses. In the larger firms, the particular division in question may be small. It may even be an insignificant part of the total enterprise.

In this event, management at the top may not know enough about the business or care enough to go through the trauma of putting forth the effort for survival. Generally, selling-off or shutdown is the easy way for large, multinational firms. The corporate office may view the business from the larger perspective much like looking through a telescope backwards.

Regardless of the conditions, there are many companies that need to take corrective actions rapidly in a downturn in order to survive, to remain viable, and to maintain credibility in the marketplace.

The situation is one of crisis management. Results must be improved quickly to stop losses. Major surgery is required. In general, the actions required involve high risks with relatively few options or alternatives.

15

EXECUTIVE AWARENESS

For the company in crisis or approaching one, the storm clouds may be gathering. Yet, the executives may be blissfully unaware or fail to acknowledge the symptoms.

The existing management seldom understands the seriousness of the situation. The managers tend to operate under the illusion that somehow sales will pick up, costs will come down in the future, products will get better, and all will be well when the general economy improves. Without exception, the idea these managers have of the time frame required to accomplish these changes is much smaller than actually required. They tend to continually look beyond the situation which exists now. Their forecasts always show improvements in the medium or long range.

Managers in businesses approaching a crisis seldom acknowledge that the existing management is inadequate. Such managers tend to believe that, with a few changes, existing personnel will be up to the task. Somehow, business managers conveniently overlook the fact that trouble really starts at the top. It starts with management.

Managers in trouble most frequently do not properly look ahead nor adequately estimate the magnitude of losses. These losses can be huge and include:

a. Large inventory markdowns.
b. Massive changes in products.
c. Extensive losses in accounts receivable.
d. Significant management changes.
e. Relearning all the way down to the supervisor level.
f. Revision of the product mix.
g. Change in customer base or channels of distribution.

Only when the executives are aware of the crisis, and only when they have agreed upon the approaching storm, can work be undertaken to turn the enterprise around.

STUDY THE ORGANIZATION

The design and implementation of organizational strategy is a major task of managers. In order to restructure the business to be cost competitive, managers must classify their competition. Competition can be classified (Chapter Six) into categories, such as:

1. Large firms with brand image, national coverage, relatively high fixed cost, and complexity.
2. High sales volume, mass market, relatively simplified with a medium range of fixed cost.
3. Regional firms with limited product range, small geographical radius, and low fixed cost.

In those cases where regional firms can take a significant share of a market, it may force the Category 1 firms to reorganize their businesses into regional ones simply to remain cost effective. This is particularly the case where brand image is not a factor and the industry is so fragmented that no one firm or relatively few firms can influence sales.

As distribution costs increase (partly due to higher fuel and operating costs for physical movement of merchandise) Category 3, or regional firms' cost competitiveness, becomes a distinct advantage over Category 1, or national firms' utilizing internal trucking and outlying warehouses, for distribution over large geographic areas.

Business Organization

Some companies operate very effectively with no organizational chart at all. Others operate with rather rigid forms of organization; but, in both cases, management must thoroughly understand the organization, how it works, and why it works.

The tendency is for organizational techniques to swing back and forth from centralization to decentralization regularly like a pendulum on a clock. As the business grows, operations and functions are centralized with complicated, heavy infrastructure and organization. Then, when profits decline, decentralization is implemented to reduce nonproductive costs in headquarters offices and services, as well as related questionable expenses.

Within the organizational structure, the business organization may be as displayed in Figure 2–1. Here, a base of manufacturing exists to manufacture

FIGURE 2–1

Business Organization

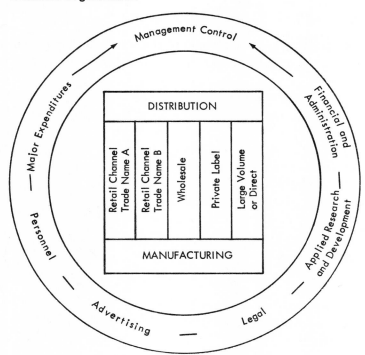

products which may be sold through multiple channels of distribution—retail, wholesale, private label, large volume, or direct sales.

The trade channels would be the channels of distribution—retail, wholesale, or others. Merchandise would be transferred at manufacturing cost to the profit centers. This could include internally manufactured products or those purchased from outside suppliers. The profit center management would be responsible for adding the appropriate profit requirement based on investments in manufacturing, distribution, and other aspects of the firm. This does require the establishment of well engineered standards for manufacturing which are relative to those attainable by competition.

The trade channels or profit centers would be responsible for financial results through operating profit at standard cost. Any variances existing in manufacturing, distribution, or other cost centers would be a responsibility of the total business.

Firm Organization

A typical chart for a business (in more detail) may be as indicated in Figure 2–2. In this case, the Sales Department is responsible for all activities related to selling and customer contact. Merchandising and Product Planning handles all functions associated with the products and making a program available to Manufacturing and Sales.

Once Merchandising and Product Planning has completed product specifications, Manufacturing is responsible for placing finished goods into the warehouse. Then, Distribution Services handles all functions from order entry to delivery, including production and inventory control.

Administration directs all the financial and administrative functions. International Sales is responsible for all shipments outside the home market.

It is important to note in the chart that there is no department, such as, "Manufacturing Services." Every activity is productive or should be eliminated. There is no such thing as "line and staff functions." Every person, every function is productive and action oriented. Typical of this line direction is the term, "Merchandising and Product Planning." There is no "Marketing Department."

The marketing concept is excellent. Yet, too many firms have created Marketing Departments and looked upon this function as the answer to their problems. Too often, no change was implemented that significantly affected customer service or the business results. Marketing is not a block on the organizational chart, or a department. It is the way of life of the firm which serves its customers—from the telephone operator to the delivery driver.

Through the years, industrial managers have adopted new terms or techniques (management science, operations research, and others), acquired new technology (electronic data processing), and spent huge sums for which insignificant improvement in business performance resulted relative to the cost.

There is no magic organizational chart. Organizational structures do not operate firms. In some cases, rigid organizations and isolated functions have

FIGURE 2–2

An Organizational Chart

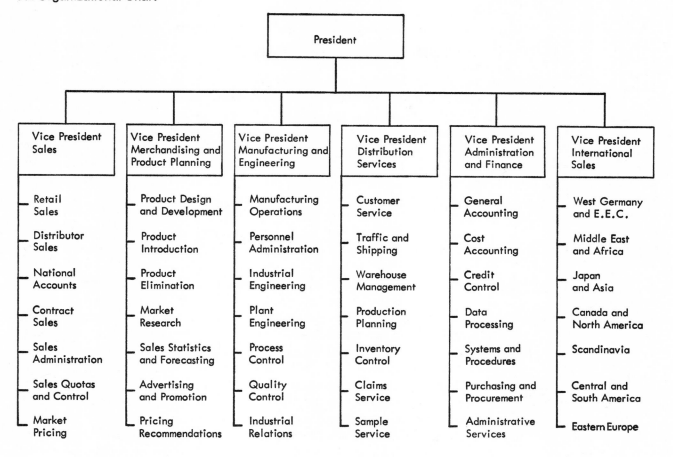

been a serious handicap to progress, individual satisfaction, and the ability to respond to changes. Flexibility is required to meet the ever-accelerating pace of business.

It will take some time to evaluate the business, its people, its markets and competition in order to arrive at an organizational structure which will be compatible and effective during the short-term turnaround. This need not be a final organization. It can be changed as business conditions require.

There are no two companies or situations which have the same organizational structure requirements. In essence, the organizational structure must exist to expedite and execute decisions. It must insure control of the business and establish clearly each manager's area of responsibility and authority. This does not mean that each and every function must be defined and shown on a chart. The fashion business, high technology industries, and others find it difficult to adequately define their structure. This is particularly true when businesses involving artists, designers, and other creative personnel involve complex interrelationships between various groups in the organization which are difficult to define in chart form.

Often, the actual organization will differ from the one set out on the company charts. This is particularly true for firms in crises, businesses requiring turnaround management, and young companies. The future character and direction of the enterprise may be unknown; it may lack specific definition or authority; it may require reversal even in this near future as the markets, competition, and financial conditions change.

Whether a manager is evaluating an existing organization or managing an established one, he must be carefully on the lookout for informal organizations which exist outside the defined organizational chart. A chart such as Figure 2–2 indicates that all vice presidents are on a similar basis with equal authority. These executives—and even lower middle level managers—build up power in a variety of ways. This power could be the result of family connections, cliques in the firm, internal politics, or other relationships.

Power management deals with fears, hopes, and expectations of weaker people. Those employing informal power exploit the weaknesses, shortcomings, and fears of others in the business. Frequently, executives employing power management are ego sensitive. These managers may be playing games. They may place their own well-being above that of the company.

In any business where one or more managers are employing harmful power advantages, this influence must be eliminated. It must not be allowed to develop within a business. Systematic, analytical, and professional management cannot be employed successfully where irrational and self-centered power management is allowed to continue. The question of power in leadership must be settled and eliminated before methodical techniques of management can be effective.

Organizations should evolve and develop on a continuing basis as the firm grows in size and complexity. Organization must change as the personnel available vary. Organizational structures need to be revised as the firm shifts from one market to another, from one sales channel to a different one, or for many other reasons.

IMPLEMENTING ORGANIZATIONAL CHANGE

The job of a manager is to run factories or fire someone. Therein lies the biggest myth in business—that progress can be made through organizational change, in the short term.

Where management of the business is incompetent, it is necessary to make organizational changes in the short term. If present management fails to comprehend the existing or approaching crisis, management must be changed.

Limited key management from the outside enables a company to make rapid progress in the short term. External recruitment brings medium- and longer-term progress after indoctrination. An individual or a manager may be known by everyone in the firm to be a disaster and a hindrance to progress. This person must be replaced.

Sometimes, changes are necessary simply to wake up the organization in total. The termination of one person often is a threat to the security of others which motivates improved performance.

The job of management is to stay in business. The best fringe benefit available to an employee at any level is a continuing business on a viable financial basis with adequate security.

In the short term, however, the key to improving results quickly includes more effective utilization of the existing personnel in the firm. To obtain someone from the outside or even relocate a person internally involves a period of transition and learning. The person being relocated or transferred cannot perform effectively for a long time due to the discontinuity.

Very frequently, people are available in the firm who can do the job required. In most cases, people want to do a good job; it is management's responsibility to give them the opportunity. Usually, when people are brought in from the outside, it simply causes additional organizational turmoil. A person who may have been overlooked sees his opportunity for promotion stopped. Then, this person begins looking for a job elsewhere—and finds it!

There is always a time lag between upsetting an organization and loss of key personnel. Some personnel begin looking for other jobs and find them 6 to 12 months later. Most likely, the people who may leave the firm are those who are needed the most when the turnaround is completed and stability has returned.

Although internal promotion is good for a company's morale, excessive promotion from within breeds shortsightedness coupled with total acceptance of senior management's role without the essential constructive criticism.

The best way to improve short-term operations is to utilize the existing people more effectively. This can be done on a planned, systematic basis by analyzing each person as indicated in Figure 2–3. This illustration is for management. Similar analyses could be performed throughout the organization.

It is management's responsibility to periodically evaluate and list each person's strengths, weaknesses, and management potential. With encouragement, motivation, and proper training, existing people can perform at a higher and more effective level. Each person must be encouraged to set objectives and list a time table for achieving these objectives.

Most people want to do good work and contribute to the success of the firm. The job of management is to allow them the opportunity. The important question is, "What can this person do well?" Then, managers must permit this person to perform in their area of strengths and move away from their weaknesses.

An abundant number of personnel changes—terminations, relocations, employment from the outside—can be eliminated. Often, people are promoted to jobs for which they have not been prepared. Then, they are fired or trans-

FIGURE 2–3

Analysis of Management

Name Position	Strengths	Weaknesses	Management Potential Opportunity to Contribute	Training and Development Needs
Bill Jones	1. Analyzes his problems and takes decisive action 2. Strong in financial administrative management 3. Well liked and communicates verbally with his personnel 4. Cost conscious and controls expenses	1. Too easy-going with his people 2. Fails to properly write and document activities 3. Fails to properly evaluate people, causing excessive terminations and transfers	1. In the short term, vice president 2. In the long term, executive vice president	1. Handling, dealing with, and evaluating people 2. Advanced business management school to broaden knowledge in total business 3. Needs experience in marketing, sales, and customer contacts

ferred. *This is the big failure of management in the free enterprise system in America.*

When a person fails (whether it is on the factory floor, in the sales field, or in management), it is a failure at the supervisory, management, or executive level. People perform best in a calm personnel environment where there is confidence and security. Constant personnel turmoil and uncertainty are the sand in the business drive shaft which lead to lower efficiency. Continuing change causes confusion and irritation among people at all levels.

When new management is brought into a firm or takes over a business through acquisition, the new managers or new owners tend to feel no responsibility for the people who have been with the firm for a number of years and who have often devoted their lives to this particular business. In restructuring, a balanced perspective of fairness and empathy is required. People's livelihoods are at stake. Their families may be uprooted. Not everyone in the business is responsible for the unfortunate condition of the enterprise. People are very nervous during a period of transition.

It is important that only a limited number of changes in key positions be made to bring order out of chaos promptly. Too many moves too quickly will result in the loss of key personnel. The situation may deteriorate rather than improve. In the short term, the real need is to find those few people in the organization who will have a real impact on improving results.

Wherever organizational changes are desired, a methodical approach is required. Too often, individual operations, divisions, and businesses are riddled with rumors and indecision. People spend most of their time talking about what may happen and worrying about changes in situations which may not even exist.

When an organizational change or personnel move is necessary, every individual concerned should be informed immediately, before he or she hears about it at the coffee machine. People should not be left with doubt. Families have been ruined, and people have had nervous breakdowns and ulcers as a result of acquisitions, division reorganizations, and individual job relocations.

In turnaround management, those changes which must be made should be handled without delay. It is necessary to develop job security for those people who will remain. Improving and utilizing the people we already have, rather than constantly changing, is a good way to improve short-term financial results.

As a rule, a company in crisis does not have good information systems. Therefore, much of the analysis will be empirical and decisions will be based on the manager's experience. The facts on which to make decisions may not be available. The changes required are generic. Structural modifications are needed. Hostility will develop from those in the firms whose positions and jobs are in jeopardy.

REVERSING POOR PERFORMANCE

The decisions which are required will carry huge risks. A balance will be required between the company's capability, its people, its financial resources, its manufacturing facilities, its customers, its markets, and its product mix.

Successful turnaround management, or reversing poor performance, is a delicate balance for management. Changes must be executed properly. There is always the possibility that "the operation was a success, but the patient died." The situation involves major surgery; it requires high risks; however, there are no alternatives for a company in crisis.

Once the health of the business enterprise has been determined, the organization restructured, and the personnel aligned, management then moves to the details of improving short-term results. These include:

1. Product planning—Chapter Three
2. Cost calculations—Chapter Four
3. Expense control—Chapter Five
4. Pricing and product mix—Chapter Six
5. Inventory management—Chapter Seven
6. Profit improvement—Chapter Eight
7. Spin-off and acquisition—Chapter Nine
8. Money management—Chapter Ten

Managers should:

Determine the degree of "crisis" in the business or severity of the approaching poor performance.

Evaluate every person on a systematic and objective basis.

RECOMMENDA-TIONS TO IMPROVE SHORT-TERM FINANCIAL MANAGEMENT

Design and implement an organizational strategy consistent with the business and restructure to meet the competition.

Make the necessary changes without delay.

Watch out for those in positions of power through relationships outside the organizational chart—family, friends, cliques in the firm, and others.

Not consider all decisions permanent. Some actions may be expendable in the short term or reversible in the long term to insure survival now.

Minimize the employment of outside personnel and utilize internal people on a more effective basis.

Slow and stop relocations which do not contribute to short-term improvement, thereby reducing relocation expenses and building organizational security.

SUMMARY

The initial procedure in turnaround management is assessing the state of the business, its management, its people, and organization.

A marginal company in good economic conditions will be one in a crisis during a downturn in the business cycle. Indeed, the crisis can occur at a frightening rate. In a poor economic environment, the poorly performing business can quickly—very quickly—face bankruptcy or financial restructuring.

Although the degrees of severity vary from firm to firm and business to business, there is a need for corrective action in the short term in virtually every business—particularly in times of cyclical economic decline. In many cases, major surgery is required involving high risks with few alternatives.

An important early step in turnaround management is for existing executives or new management to be fully aware of the severity of the crisis. In many cases, existing management fails to understand the seriousness of the situation. These managers tend to underestimate the change required, the losses which may occur, and the time required to improve results. Problems start with management, management at the top. And, existing management seldom acknowledges that present personnel are inadequate.

For a poorly performing business, large losses can occur in inventory write-downs, massive changes in products, accounts receivable, and other aspects of the business. Only when executives are aware of the magnitude of the crisis, and only when they agree that there is an approaching storm, can work be undertaken to turn the enterprise around.

For the firm in crisis or for any business, the primary job of managers is to take those actions which will permit the business to survive.

The design and implementation of an organizational strategy is an essential task of management. It is necessary to classify the firm relative to competition before beginning restructuring. Methods of classifying competition are contained in this chapter.

A typical organizational chart is displayed. There is no such thing as "line and staff functions." Every person, every function, is productive and action oriented or it should be eliminated. Management techniques which do not contribute to improved results should be discarded.

Managers must be alert to informal organizations which exist outside the organizational chart. These often involve the accumulation of informal power by individuals or groups formed through friends, cliques in the firm, family associations, or other relationships. These informal organizations will handicap the improvement of operations. They may destroy new managers and prevent their objectives from being achieved. These harmful power groups must be eliminated.

Management changes are necessary to replace incompetent managers, to wake up an organization, and to bring a sense of urgency to every person in the business. In many situations, capable people are in the firm who would like to contribute to its success; it is management's job to give them the opportunity.

Changes which are required should be planned on a systematic basis and implemented quickly. Otherwise, individual operations, divisions, and businesses will be riddled with rumors and indecision. Developing a sense of security for those who will remain and contribute to improved performance is essential for a successful turnaround in operations.

Where a firm is under pressure to improve results, managers may not have time and data may not be available with sufficient accuracy to pinpoint permanent decisions. Short-term decisions which are expendable may be required. These actions which enable survival of the business in the short term may be reversible in the long term.

Turnaround management does not involve tinkering with the business or tuning up existing operations. Many of the decisions are generic. Most of the changes are structural in nature. There are generally few or limited options for a company in crisis. The decisions are major; the risks are high. The changes are necessary in order to insure survival in the short term or there will be no business to strategically plan for in the long range time frame.

chapter THREE

Product Explosion

To get higher sales volume, give us more products to match competition.

Solving the Riddle of Complexity

A SYSTEMATIC, organized, and methodical approach to product planning can release millions of dollars, finance added sales, delay the time required to build new plants and facilities, and reduce the need for cash. Simplified products with lower manufacturing costs can reduce complexity. Funds saved can lower interest payments and improve effectiveness throughout the firm. Product planning is a key opportunity to improve short-term financial management.

Management may be critical of manufacturing for higher costs and lower efficiencies. In many cases, inventories may be too high. Losses on discontinued and obsolete merchandise may be excessive.

Frequently, these losses in effectiveness are created by complexity. Complexity in products causes transactions which increase costs. These show up in excessive product changes, short unit runs, and higher administrative expenses. The starting point for effectiveness is the orderly approach to product planning.

This requires a method which employs the fewest possible products to be manufactured from the minimum different raw materials, assembly parts, or components. These must allow flexibility to provide the widest range of customer products and consumer needs.

Simplification of the product mix enables the people in the factory to concentrate on learning the job and building a better product. It permits customer service to direct its efforts on the fewest products and improve service levels.

Sometimes, it appears that higher sales require more and more products and stockkeeping items—sizes, colors, package variations, and other complexities. A systematic approach is required to sort out those few products, those few colors, and those few packages which contribute to profit. Noncontributors to the firm's marketing strategies must be eliminated unless these are required to balance a line of products—colors, sizes, or other needs. Some items can be "Planned Product Specialties."

Creative research and development personnel and product style and design oriented personnel concentrate on interesting product designs, rather than

29

on those which can be produced efficiently with proper product quality and within the limitations of production equipment. Effective product planning requires participative management—a team effort of the Research and Development Department, style and design personnel, marketing, sales, manufacturing, and administrative personnel. When product planning departments or engineering units are allowed to operate in a vacuum, isolated from other functions, complexity is created and transactions are generated which cannot be overcome on the factory floor.

Several guides which exist to help determine product value are sales volume, profitability, contribution, and others. Most of these relate to some past history or statistical data.

The majority of manufacturing enterprises today are capital intensified. As industries become more automated, more sophisticated, and have higher cost installations, the productivity lost due to product changes and other forms of complexity can be enormous. Funds required to maintain finished inventories, work-in-process, raw materials, and accounts receivable can exceed the value of the capital investment.

As complexity increases, more extensive data processing systems and other service costs are required to insure continuous production and availability of information.

None of these added costs are recoverable as they do not perform a service to the customer. Every aspect which causes cost must contribute some real value added in the market, either real or intangible. The adding of cost to produce, control, and service complex or unreasonable activities reduces profits which cannot be recovered in the marketplace.

More effective utilization of high cost installations can be achieved with accurate sales forecasting and production and inventory control systems. Systematic and simplified product planning enables these systems to function with more efficiency and reliability.

Sometimes, in visiting trade shows and in reading industry publications, it seems that new ideas and new products are the way to success. In many cases, this is correct. Yet, the vast majority of financial results can be improved by a businesslike approach to improving the effectiveness of existing products.

It is not always necessary to be first in the market, except in the case of high technology or completely new products. When problems must be worked out of basic manufacturing processes, it may be best to be second or third into the market with certain new ideas.

Though it may seem like heresy in the world of management, short-term financial management can best be achieved by improving the utilization of existing products and resources. This must be done without affecting the long-term reliability of the firm.

For a company in crisis, the need for short-term results may mean sacrificing what may be best for long-range product planning. The need for survival can justify the short-term strategy of cutting back existing or new products.

Management is not always a movement forward. Sometimes, a step backward is necessary to stay in business in order to move ahead later. Regardless of the excellent ideas in the line or under development, certain creditors may not wish to advance the funds to finance added inventories or stockkeeping items. Distributors, retailers, and other customers may not be in a position to finance new products. Sometimes, management must put the house in order today or there will be no "next season."

An organized approach to product planning can improve short-term financial management by:

1. Reducing the buildup of inventories or supplies required for new products (this can quickly reduce the cash required in many businesses by millions of dollars).
2. Eliminating the need for expensive new equipment or plant modifications which can reduce cash requirements plus increase the productivity of existing facilities.
3. Lowering the cost on samples, sales promotion, and advertising expense (this expense can easily be reduced to 1 to 2 percent, whereas, many firms have as much as 3 to 4 percent of this expense component).
4. Cutting the loss on obsolete and discontinued merchandise, disposing of miscellaneous inventories, and taking the resulting losses immediately.
5. Lowering the amount of off-quality items produced which will cut cost and take this merchandise out of the market where it is causing pressure to reduce prices.
6. Diminishing the money required throughout the entire channel of distribution—manufacturing, retail or distributor, parts supplier, or other chain in the channel of distribution (a superior firm with superior results will not have more than 1 to 2 percent interest cost).

SYSTEMATIC APPROACH

To get a quick or continuing evaluation of existing or new product ideas, managers must utilize systematic evaluation techniques in addition to historical methods using sales volume, contribution, or profits. Management is knowledge—knowledge of the market, knowledge of technology, and knowledge of competition as conditions continually change. Management is judgment.

Analytical methods can reduce the range of decision error. Most decisions are a selection of one course of action from a series of alternatives based on opinions. Extensive market research could not predict the failure of the Edsel, nor the overwhelming success of the Mustang. In the final analysis, introduction of new products is a blending of analytical information and management intuition coupled with management's knowledge of the market.

A typical classification system for products is displayed in Figure 3–1. In product planning meetings, in order to evaluate products objectively, a classification system of this or a similar type is necessary.

Then, a list of each change which is required can be prepared and docu-

FIGURE 3–1

Product Classification

Classification	Description
1	*Present Earners:* Products which generate an important share of total sales, usually 10 percent or more, fall into this category. These are products with some room for growth. A downward price change may be required due to competition or other reasons. Present Earners have a profit margin not less than that of the average for the total product line.
2	*Future Earners:* These products may be new introductions with the potential for a higher profit margin than the average product mix. They will have a higher inventory turnover potential than that presently being achieved. Normally, these products will have customer appeal, style, color, or other attributes which will help them sell themselves.
3	*Planned Product Specialties:* Included in this classification are products, colors, or packages which may be small in sales volume. Yet, they serve a useful function for marketing—high quality products to build an image in the product mix, color required for selection, or specialty items. Generally, the profit margin per unit is well above that of the overall product mix.
4	*Promotional Items:* These products would generally be lower priced items to gain entry to a customer, to compete in a specific market area, or to be used for sales promotion. The profit margin would be lower than that of the overall product mix. An item in the Promotional Items would be moved up in price upon completion of the promotion.
5	*Commodity Products:* Products in this category would be standard items usually sold in large volume to meet mass competition. Commodity Products would not normally have any technological, style, or other unique appeal. These items would not have the profit margin of the overall product mix. These products could be in the line to use idle capacity or recover fixed cost.
6	*Obsolete:* These may be either high volume or low volume products which are creating cost, low profit margins, or special considerations. Products classified as Obsolete should be discontinued at the end of the model year or other time interval. Inventories should be minimized as the product is phased out.
7	*Yesterday's Earners:* Products declining in volume or profit margin fall into this classification. These items should be phased out of the line in the short term. Systematic product planning will have a replacement available for these items.

FIGURE 3–1 *(continued)*

Classification	Description
8	*Overlooked Earners:* These products are characterized by sales and profit margin in excess of expectations with very little effort on the part of sales or management. They could be mispriced, underestimated, incorrectly evaluated, or be appealing to the wrong trade channels or customers. Products in this category should be exploited to their maximum potential. Action must be taken to move them in the direction of Present Earners or Future Earners.
9	*Modification Needed:* In almost every business there are some products which are moving along at a normal or average sales volume. With modification these could be moved into Classification 1—Present Earners, or Classification 2—Future Earners. They may fall into the following general pattern:
	a. Products with a present sales volume of less than 5 percent of total sales could be modified.
	b. Modified products should have growth opportunities. The product should have a recognized value in the market.
	c. The product requires only a minor modification or marketing change to put it into Classification 1—Present Earners.

Source: Adapted from Peter F. Drucker, *Managing for Results* (New York: Harper & Row, 1964), pp. 51–67.

mented similar to Figure 3–2. As an example, a typical product may be in Classification 8—Overlooked Earners. It may be that this product was mispriced and a change in the pricing will enable it to be upgraded to Classification 1—Present Earners.

Obsolete products should be uncovered quickly to improve short-term results. These items should be disposed of without delay. There is often

FIGURE 3–2

Classification of Products and Life Cycle

Product		Present Class	Present Product Life Cycle		Modification Required	Potential Class	Potential Product Life Cycle	
No.	Name		Profit	Volume			Profit	Volume
1230	Fancy Living...	8	A	C	Revise colors........	2	A	A
1441	Caravelle......	1	B	B	Promotion and pricing to extend life cycle.	6	C	C

Note: A = Trending upward; B = Level; C = Trending downward.

nothing to be gained by holding such items while they create inventory costs. The loss, if any, most frequently should be taken *now* on the Profit and Loss Statement. The cash that can be obtained could be utilized for other purposes —to pay off debts, or to improve liquidity.

Overlooked Earners, in the short term, should be carefully studied. If long or expensive advertising, promotion, or modification is required, these will not contribute to improved results quickly. In fact, they may be a liability or risk which is outside the narrow range within which management must operate in a time of crisis.

This method permits the manager to define the action needed and designate the person responsible. A deadline to achieve the objective is required. Then, follow-up is necessary to insure that decisions and actions are implemented.

PRODUCT LIFE CYCLE

To maintain simplification of products, maximize the investment in research and development, and optimize production facilities, the product life cycle is a valuable opportunity for management.

Generally, new products have high profit and low volume as indicated in Figure 3–3. As additional competitors come on the market, volume may increase both for the developer of the product and competition. Normally, competitive conditions will bring down the profit per unit. However, the effective marketer can use techniques to extend the product life cycle.

A product may be introduced at a relatively high price in Stage I (Figure 3–3) and be declining into Stage II. At the proper time, a manufacturer may well change the pricing policy or introduce new products or accessories to move the profit per unit life cycle upward.

Another view of the product life cycle is contained in Figure 3–4. In this case, the normal life cycle begins with relatively low volume and increases as market acceptance and production capacity become available. The leveling portion of the life cycle between Stages B and D may last for some years or even be as short as a few months or a market season. An automobile model may be on the market for years, whereas a clothing or apparel fabric style may last for six months or less.

By charting the product life cycles, management can keep abreast of changing trends. New products can be introduced at the proper time. New colors, new patterns, or new designs will extend the life cycle of the basic product as indicated by the dotted line shown in Figure 3–4.

Extensions of life cycles are very effective ways of maximizing profitability and return on investment all the way through the trade channels. Samples on the market can generate more sales dollars per dollar investment with an extended life cycle. Spare parts in repair shops and distribution of manufacture inventories can be utilized more fully. Production equipment can produce more parts with the same initial investment by extending the life cycle.

FIGURE 3–3

Product Profit and Volume Life Cycle

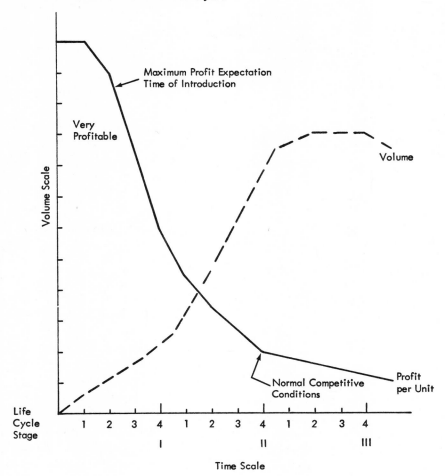

As with forecasting and financial analysis, it is the change in trend or potential change in trend which is important. These changes must be detected at an early stage in order to improve performance in advance.

A key to having a minimum number of products in the system is analyzing the products available versus end use or market demand. A typical product line analysis of prices and end uses for a typical consumer goods product is indicated in Figure 3–5.

The existing products may be plotted into price points and end use tables of this type. In this manner, the Product Development or Engineering Departments can determine when they have too many products for a given

MINIMUM PRODUCTS FOR MAXIMUM MARKET COVERAGE

FIGURE 3–4

Product Life Cycle

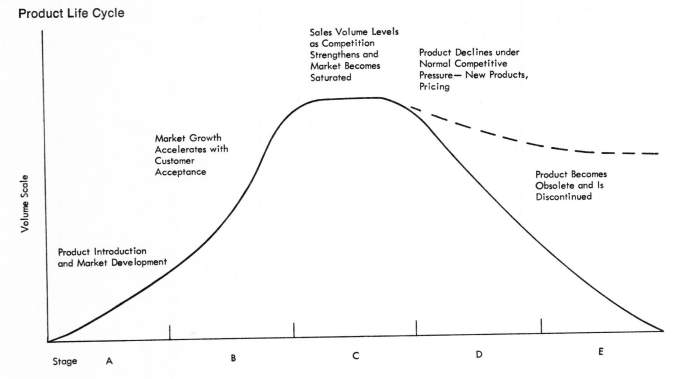

end use or their products are concentrated too much into a particular price point.

As an example, the products may be well suited for conventional bedrooms, but the size and special requirements for mobile homes may have been omitted. Likewise, the products could be offered too heavily in the lower priced and smaller contribution price points.

Of course, products must be bunched into the mass market price points to insure sufficient volume and unit runs. A typical example of office equipment or furniture of a price point curve by volume is shown in Figure 3–6.

A similar diagram can be prepared of a particular business' sales and products versus the available market or industry. This can show where additional products are needed and where some can be phased out of the line.

Charts of this type are usually based on sales volume in units or sales volume in dollars. Very frequently, the profitability per unit curve is inversely related to the volume—the higher the sales volume, the lower the unit profit or contribution to fixed cost and profits.

A key to determining the products required by price point is the income elasticity of demand for the product, both in the short term and the long term. This factor can guide product changes. As an example, products can be segregated into three categories:

1. Highly sensitive areas.
2. Average sensitivity areas.
3. Relatively insensitive areas.

Certain products based on habit, such as tobacco, are believed to be necessary to serve an individual's habitual desire. These may be relatively insensitive to small price changes in both the short term and the long term. Therefore, little increased volume could be expected by developing a product which would result in a lower price. Volume might be increased by producing a package size with lower content and a lower price. Large price changes, such as doubling the price or cutting the price in half, could change the sensitivity of any product over both the short and long term.

FIGURE 3–5

Product Line Analysis: Price and End Use

Retail Price Range	End Uses							
	Bedroom	Kitchen	Bathroom	Game room	Outdoor Area	Mobile Home	Offices	Commercial Areas
Up to $59.50								
$59.50 to $69.50								
$69.50 to $79.50								
$79.50 to $89.50								
$89.50 to $99.50								
$99.50 to $109.50								
$109.50 to $119.50								
Over $119.50								

Products which have a wear-out life (as an example, footwear) may be of average sensitivity to short-term price increases and relatively insensitive to long-term changes.

Household appliances—washing machines, radios, and similar items—may be highly sensitive to short-term price changes and of average sensitivity to long-term price changes. In this situation, the producer, the distributor, and the retailer would capitalize on a person's desire for an item which is fulfilled by a promotion or promotional price, promotional product, or immediate purchase response.

Many products fall into the category of postponable consumer goods purchases. Postponable purchases can sometimes be substituted by consumer trading down decisions. Floor coverings, furniture, and similar items with

FIGURE 3–6

Sales Distribution by Price Point

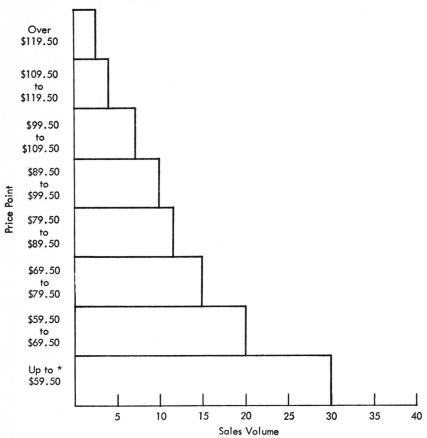

* Including sales and promotions under $59.50.

reasonably large value per unit of purchase fall into this category. Products and prices must be evaluated based on price and income elasticity.

Figure 3–7 is an example of some of the products and their expectations relative to sensitivity in the short term and long term.

For short-term improvement, there is not much to be gained by reducing prices except to be competitive on products which are long-term sensitive to price changes. Price reductions, rebate schemes, and other gimmicks shift sales from one time period to another. No firm has an advantage. Such techniques will simply be adopted by other competitors.

Care must be exercised in reducing prices even on those items which are price sensitive in the short term. Price reductions at the manufacturing level are usually lost in the distribution channels or add inventory which will result in lost sales later. Methods must be employed which insure that any price reduction is passed on to the end-using customer.

FIGURE 3–7

Effect of Price and Income Elasticity

	Short Term	Long Term
Highly Sensitive		
	Household appliances	Furniture and furnishings
	Furniture and furnishings	Floor covering
	Transportation (automobiles, motorcycles, etc.)	Medical and pharmaceutical supplies
	Men's and boy's clothing	Purchase transportation (taxi's, airlines, etc.)
	Recreational products	
Average Sensitivity		
	Footwear	Household appliances
	Floor covering	Transportation (automobiles, motorcycles, etc.)
	Jewelry	Recreational products
	Purchase transportation (taxi's, airlines, etc.)	Jewelry
	Women's and children's clothing	Tobacco products
Relatively Insensitive		
	Food products	Footwear
	Tobacco products	Women's and children's clothing
	Alcoholic beverages	Men's and boy's clothing
	Medical and pharmaceutical supplies	Alcoholic beverages
		Food products

MAXIMIZING DISTRIBUTION

The key to long unit runs on the factory floor is maximizing distribution with basic components. A typical product explosion to maximize basic assembly operations is indicated in Figure 3–8.

By drawing product diagrams of this type, Product Planning can see where a gap exists in the market. Further, the Marketing and Sales Departments can determine which trade channels are not being properly serviced. These charts can show the various types of containers which can be utilized to maximize a distribution process plus fill gaps in the market requirements and price points.

MANUFACTURING PROCESS MAXIMIZATION

In assembly, a continuous process industry, or other method of technology, a manufacturing process system exists which is difficult to interrupt. In this case, the manufacturing process and raw materials system must be maximized.

A diagram of a typical manufacturing process explosion is shown in Figure 3–9. Here, flexibility to serve a wide range of customer needs, price point, and trade channels can be obtained with a relatively rigid manufacturing process.

FIGURE 3–8

Product Explosion
(broaden distribution, maximize production, and minimize inventory risk)

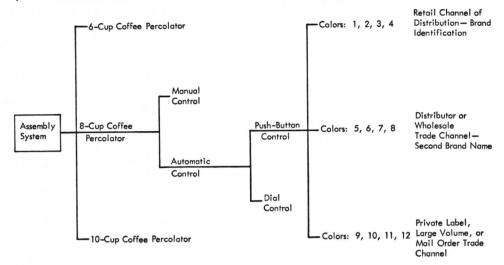

As new facilities are planned in today's rapidly changing world, the key factor, even at a higher capital cost, is maintaining the opportunity for flexibility in materials, processes, and products to meet unforeseen demands in the years ahead.

An analysis of this type can point up areas where product modifications can utilize the existing assembly or manufacturing processes more effectively. Improving the utilization of existing facilities is a key opportunity for improving short-term financial management. Further, output expansions from present factories and equipment can postpone the time required for major capital expenditures.

FIGURE 3–9

Manufacturing Process Explosion
(maximize production and broaden product end use applications)

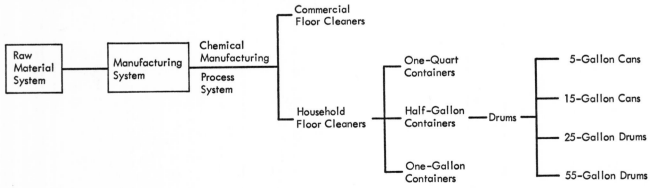

An important key to maintaining simplification is controlling new product introductions—either sizes, completely new products, colors, or any elements which create a new stockkeeping unit.

A typical form for controlling new introductions is shown in Figure 3–10. In this case, the proposal is introduced and approved by various management executives.

It is important to note that Manufacturing must review the new product before it is introduced. Often, manufacturing personnel can recommend a slight change which will reduce cost, or process engineers can come up with new processing methods to increase productivity or quality. In many cases, full-scale production runs are required to insure success in manufacturing with a new product.

Likewise, the Controller's Department or financial executive must determine the investment in inventory, inventory turns, and capital employed to put the new product into production and distribution.

After all executives have used their knowledge and experience to evaluate a product system, it can then be properly approved for introduction with full support of all executives and functions of the business.

It is much easier to get a new product into production than it is to get an old product out. Management must always set stockkeeping unit targets. When these are exceeded, products should be eliminated.

Products in Classification 6—Obsolete must be eliminated. The constant turnover of products is required to maintain current marketability of the product range.

When a product has been dropped from sales, it should be completely discontinued. Often, management will discontinue a product; yet, salesmen will continue to take orders which require short unit runs, spare parts, or other resource needs.

Very frequently, a new product will be initiated and fail quickly. In an effort to avoid embarrassment, management will use too much of its resources (time, advertising, and finances) to make it a success. Management must recognize and accept failure. It is better to take an early loss than to continue efforts to market an unsatisfactory product, package, or other item.

The discontinuing of products must be planned in advance to minimize inventory losses. After a product is classified and planned to be eliminated, the available inventory or finished goods, work-in-process, and raw materials should be evaluated. Special sales promotions should be initiated to eliminate these inventories to avoid markdowns before the product is finally eliminated.

To reduce inventories and costs for discontinuing a product, sales may be terminated in many geographical areas or with most customers. Then, one or two trading areas, or a selected few customers, can continue to be sold a product pending a reduction in inventory. Elimination of inventories of slow moving or discontinued products at a profit is a key to systematic and pro-

FIGURE 3–10

Application for New Product
(change of product, additional stockkeeping items, or other modifications)

Date _____   No. _____

I. VICE PRESIDENT MERCHANDISING AND SALES
   Product Name _____ Product Number _____
   Description of Competitive Products and Price _____
   _____
   Primary Material Required _____
   Secondary Material Required _____
   Total Number of Stockkeeping Units _____
   Reason for Request _____
   Method of Distribution: 1. Retail _____ 2. Distributor __
                            3. National Accounts __ 4. Other _____
   Annual Forecast in Units   __ Target Selling Price per Unit   __
   Date Needed for Introduction __ Expected Selling Price per Unit __

   _____   _____
   Vice President Sales   Vice President Merchandising

II. VICE PRESIDENT RESEARCH AND DEVELOPMENT
    Pilot Plant Trial Run No. _____ Factory Trial Run No. _____
    Potential Problems _____
    Recommendations and Comments _____
    _____

                   _____
                   Vice President Research and Development

III. VICE PRESIDENT MANUFACTURING
     1. Feasibility of Producing
        a. Factory Production Run Results _____
        b. Additional Trial Runs Required _____
        c. Potential Production Problems _____
        d. Potential Quality Problems _____
     2. Materials Position
        a. Primary Material Availability _____
        b. Secondary Material Availability _____
        c. Availability of Other Materials or Parts Which Could Delay
           Production _____

FIGURE 3–10 *(continued)*

3. Equipment Position
   a. Primary Production Equipment Availability _____
   b. Units per Week Required _____
   c. Additional Equipment and Cost Required _____
   d. Productivity at Critical Manufacturing Processes _____

4. Recommendations and Comments _____
   _____

   _____
   Vice President Manufacturing

IV. VICE PRESIDENT OF FINANCE

1. Estimated Investment
   a. Raw Materials $ _____
   b. Work-In-Process $ _____
   c. Finished Goods $ _____
   d. Total Capital Investment Required $ _____
2. Profitability
   a. Standard Profit at Net Selling Price $ _____
   b. Standard Variable Contribution at
      Net Selling Price $ _____
   c. Fixed Cost Recovered per Unit $ _____
   d. Estimated Units Required to Re-
      cover Capital Investment $ _____
3. Recommendations and Comments _____
   _____

   _____
   Vice President Finance

V. AUTHORIZATION FOR RELEASE TO PRODUCTION PLANNING

Recommendations and Comments _____
_____

Yes _____ No _____   _____
                                                   President

VI. VICE PRESIDENT DISTRIBUTION SERVICES

Initial Production Scheduled   _____
Initial Production Available   _____
Product Nos. and Codes Assigned _____
Inventory Available for Shipment _____

_____
Vice President Distribution Services

fessional product management. It is essential to improve results in the short term.

RECOMMENDATIONS TO IMPROVE SHORT-TERM FINANCIAL MANAGEMENT

Certain actions can be taken in the short term—within one year—to improve the utilization and productivity of people, of equipment, resources, and money without endangering the long-run capability of the firm.

Managers should:

Methodically evaluate all products to determine those which can be expanded in sales volume by product modification, pricing promotion, or other methods.

Discontinue those products which are causing cost and complexity.

Eliminate items which require excessive inventory of raw materials, work-in-process, or finished goods.

Add products which can easily be introduced to broaden distribution and to utilize facilities to reduce idle capacity.

Set up a systematic approach to new product introductions; find out the costs and problems involved before introduction.

SUMMARY

Simplified product planning on a systematic, professional basis is essential to successful business management. The techniques indicated in this chapter demonstrate systematic methods of product classification, product life cycles, and methods of maximizing price point and end use coverage.

Techniques of insuring that the largest number of trade channels can be covered with the minimum number of products are explained. Similarly, charts demonstrate how to maintain maximum productivity from continuous process, assembly line, or other rigid installations. A procedure of controlling new introductions and ways for reducing the liability resulting from discontinued products are put forth.

The cost of manufacturing facilities continues to increase. Even with decentralization, much rigidity exists in manufacturing processes. At every point, plants and facilities should be planned with the maximum flexibility to service unknown consumer demand and technological change.

Effective utilization of these high cost installations requires accurate sales forecasting, production, and inventory control. These systems—either manual, batch process, or real time automated equipment—always function more efficiently for better customer service with a simplified and stable product mix.

In analyzing the reason for poor performance, managers must always separate mechanical system's problems from those requiring a change in approach to the business. Most sophisticated systems do not replace the need for simplified product planning. Complexity, for whatever the reason, is often the cause for failure of more soundly based theoretical and professionally implemented systems.

Sometimes, managers of a business in crisis must cut back existing and excellent new products under development to survive in the short term and be ready for growth in the years ahead. In this situation, stockkeeping items and inventories must be cut back or there will be no "next season."

Price reductions must be evaluated very carefully based on the sensitivity of the product to price changes. Price changes at the manufacturing level may be absorbed in the distribution channels—distributors, large buyers, or retailers—or simply shift sales from one time period to another. Where price reductions are employed to increase sales volume, methods must be used which insure that lower cost is passed on to the final consumer.

The resources of the enterprise must be devoted to those few products which are Present Earners and Future Earners. Obsolete products must be eliminated now. Promotional Items and Commodity Products must be controlled within the limits established by managers.

section two

chapter FOUR

Cost Calculations

Cost calculations using percentages, averages, and historical data are obsolete in today's world. Using an average of any sort is like putting one foot in a hot oven and the other in a freezer. On the average, you're comfortable.

The Cause of Costs—Transactions

ONE of the characteristics common to superior managers and one of the keys to professional management is understanding costs and financial information —how a decision relates to the total business. This cannot be delegated.

There is no need to argue about costing techniques—contribution accounting, variable costing, full absorption costing, or other theories.[1] There is no purpose to be gained by using any one as the only guide. The important need is to understand these methods and what dimension each of these methods give to understanding the business.

Too often, firms rely on "profits" as the tool. Others depend on "contribution margins" as the best instrument. The fact is that managers need all the guides available to operate and control a business. A manager need not switch the management compass from one technique to another. The control system needs all the instrument points available, and once understood, each can serve a useful purpose.

None of these financial yardsticks are of value unless the cost calculations are accurate. Averages and percentages are obsolete. Costs must be engineered. They must be based on cause of costs—transactions, complexity, unit run size, and related variables.

There is a reason for every cost or it should be eliminated. That reason, then, becomes the basis for calculation by stockkeeping item, by cost center, or by trade channel.

First, obsolete or misleading terms should be eliminated. These cause confusion, particularly with newer, better trained personnel entering the firm. "Overhead" is a word which should be discarded. It is misleading and incorrect. Each cost, whether variable or fixed, is an expense which adds cost to the product. It should be identified, managed, or eliminated. "Indirect labor" is another term to be deleted. All labor is productive or unnecessary. Industrial engineering methods exist which can determine standards with

---

[1] Frank C. Wilson, *Industrial Cost Controls* (Englewood Cliffs, N.J.: Prentice-Hall, Inc., 1971), pp. 49–51.

reasonable accuracy for so-called "indirect" jobs, such as a lift truck driver, as well as for "direct" jobs on the production line.

The breaking down of labor into "direct" and "indirect" adds unnecessary complexity to payroll recording in the factory and payroll accounting in the office. Further, the use of a term like "indirect" may imply to management that this element is uncontrollable. It may cause them to de-emphasize an opportunity for reducing costs.

Although the terms or words used may seem trivial to some in the business scene, they are part of the philosophy, part of the environment of a professional firm in today's changing world.

COST SHEET INFORMATION

A cost sheet may contain the information displayed in Figure 4–1. This layout provides a somewhat different breakdown of information than that utilized by many businesses. It gives five different points to guide decisions.

FIGURE 4–1

Typical Cost Sheet Summary

Description	Cost per Packed Unit	Contribution at Standards	Decision Points*
Part A	$ 15.00		
Part B	9.50		
Part C	5.50		
Primer	1.50		
Paint	4.50		
Packaging:	9.00		
Material cost	$ 45.00	$88.00	I
Supplies and repairs	2.00		
Fuel and utilities	3.00		
Total purchases	$ 50.00	83.00	II
Cost at Process A	13.00		
Cost at Process B	5.00		
Quality losses	3.00		
Sales and distribution	7.00		
Interest—short term	2.00		
Total variable cost	$ 80.00	53.00	III
Manufacturing	8.00		
Distribution	5.00		
Research and development	2.00		
Sales	9.00		
Administration	4.00		
Interest—long term	2.00		
Total manufacturing cost Less depreciation	$110.00	16.00	IV
Depreciation	10.00		
Total Cost	$120.00		
Net Profit	6.00	6.00	V
Target price after tax	$126.00		
Provision for taxes	7.00		
Net target selling price	$133.00		
Discounts and terms	8.00		
Total Target Price	$141.00		

* See text.

I. Gross margin is the net sales price ($133.00) minus the material cost ($45.00), or $88.00.
II. Value added is the net sales price ($133.00) minus purchases—materials, fuel, utilities, supplies, and repairs ($50.00)—or $83.00.
III. Contribution margin based on direct costing theory is the contribution to fixed cost and profits. In this example, it is the net sales price ($133.00) minus the variable cost ($80.00), or $53.00.
IV. Cash flow is the after tax profit ($6.00) plus depreciation ($10.00), or $16.00.
V. After tax profits are $6.00.

This format highlights the important cost of interest, both in the short term and the long term. This is a true cost. It is one frequently overlooked and perhaps the difference between profit and loss in hard times.

Many attack full absorption costs or total cost calculations as inaccurate due to allocations and distributions. Actually, variable costing only in contribution margins is easy. With proper account definition, fixed cost elements can be determined with equal accuracy as those for variable costs.

It is true that in using total costs incorrectly errors can occur; product mix changes, volume changes, and other differences affect the validity of this information. A professional manager is not only capable of understanding these situations; he *must* know them. To use only "contribution margin" or any other one guide is similar to a pilot using only one altimeter to determine his flight conditions. As shown in Figure 4–1, managers can have all the information—gross margin, value added, contribution margin, cash flow, and net profit after tax. These give the manager the key points he needs to know to run his business effectively.

Gross margin is defined as:

Gross Margin

Gross Margin = Net Selling Price — Material Costs.

Gross margin is required so that businesses can maximize the difference between material costs and sales dollars. This is the only way a manager can maintain control and not become a conversion business with material suppliers being the dominant factor.

Managers must avoid permitting their business to become just a conversion of raw materials for sale to a few large buyers. The key to profitability is maintaining control of the business—either from a raw material or selling standpoint. In a predominantly conversion activity, the manager of the manufacturing operation finds himself in a box being squeezed ever tighter by suppliers and buyers.

Gross margin is an important key in the distribution or wholesale business. In many of these situations the material costs can be two thirds, three fourths, or even more of the total operating cost. Further, operating costs—though theoretically some may be variable—tend to be fixed. Here, a small change in gross margins (say, 1 percent) is a significant change in financial results, often, in the magnitude of 25 to 100 percent change.

The key to successful management is concentration on those few things which can have an important effect on financial results. In wholesaling, it may be material or cost of purchases. In manufacturing, it may be raw material costs. In labor intensified industries, it could be the personnel cost of production.

Value Added

The definition of value added is:

$$\text{Value Added} = \text{Net Selling Price} - \text{Purchases (Materials} + \text{Supplies} + \text{Repairs} + \text{Fuels)}.$$

Added value is needed in those countries where value added taxes are applicable, particularly in Continental Europe and Scandinavia. *Value added is a useful guide to managing a business.*

In general, by increasing the proportion of value added relative to other components or outside purchases, the manager is more likely to move his business into noncompetitive areas. As an example, a manufacturer may purchase basic raw materials and subcontract certain components. By bringing the subcontracting portion into the operations, the firm becomes more integrated and less liable to disruption by outside suppliers. Further, a manufacturer may refuse to buy his raw materials at an earlier stage of processing and perform the processing internally. This increase is value added to the firm.

The firm may have a series of products. Some of these may be of relatively simple manufacture; others may incorporate sophisticated technology. Those with simple manufacturing methods are most likely to be attacked easily by competitors. Therefore, by moving to more technologically oriented processed products or operations which require skilled personnel, a firm may increase value added and move into less competitive areas. These statements apply largely to industries where multiple competitors exist. It would not apply to very technological and highly capital intensified businesses with few competitors, such as aircraft manufacturers and others.

Value added does not necessarily imply tangible manufacturing processes or costs. Value added can include higher prices achieved in the market as a result of product uniqueness, style and design, or other intangibles for which the consumer is willing to pay a price.

As an example, consider the industry of Switzerland. Here, a nation has a relatively small population, limited geographical area, and few raw material sources. Yet, by concentrating on technologically advanced products, and those with skilled production requirements, the Swiss add a high value to the products manufactured giving a sound industrial base. It also provides one which is less vulnerable to competition.

A somewhat similar but slightly different situation exists in Japan. Geographically, the area occupied by the nation is relatively small. As contrasted with Switzerland, it does have a large population. Being isolated by water and distance from many major raw material and fuel sources, it is heavily dependent on raw materials from abroad. By developing an industrial base with high value added to the imported raw materials, by using precision in design to economize materials and by maintaining quality of production, the industry of Japan has been able to compete worldwide. This has been achieved even with the high distribution cost to the major markets for their finished products which are exported.

Value added can be a useful concept, then, for an individual business, an industry, or a national economy. The biggest disadvantage is the value added tax (VAT) now applied in many nations. Here, governments are taxing and retarding the very element or concept which could lead to success.

In France, added value for taxation purposes is defined as the difference between all purchases and total sales after deducting taxes and also social charges (which in France equal 40 percent or more of the payroll).

Contribution Margin

Utilizing direct costing, contribution margin is:

$$\text{Contribution Margin} = \text{Net Selling Price} - \text{Variable Costs.}$$

Variable costs are those which vary with production. These include purchase of materials, fuel, and other elements which vary as the quantity of production changes in volume of units or variation in operations, such as changing one shift to two shifts of production. Many items which have previously been considered variable are becoming fixed. One of these is personnel cost. It is no longer possible to lay off people on short notice. Further, it is bad policy. For short-term decisions, personnel expense in many areas is fixed.

Accounts should be defined so that they will either be fixed or variable. In some cases (electrical costs) there may be a fixed demand charge and a variable usage charge. In most of these situations, the items should be considered completely variable as the fixed portion is relatively minor. Variable should be any item which changes from three to five day operation. Where an account has a fixed portion and it is an important element, the accounts should be separated or subcoded to separate fixed and variable expenses. These should not be broken down as some percentage by the cost accountant.

There is no need to spend time arguing about what is variable or what is fixed. Some "rule of thumb" or heuristic method should be utilized where difference of opinion exists. If one wishes to get to the fact, everything is variable! Any business can be shut down completely and its assets sold.

Contribution margin is a very important guide for short-term pricing decisions. This is true particularly where idle capacity exists. The job of the manager is to understand how to use this information to an advantage, as well as the dangers! Chapter Six on Pricing explores the utilization of contribution margins for pricing in more depth and scope.

Total Costs

Total costs include all materials, variable costs, depreciation, and other fixed elements. Managers must know their total costs (given the assumptions in their business plan for volume, products, and pricing). Many cost systems provide variable costs only.

Variable or direct costing only is easy. The determination of total costs or full absorption costing requires discipline in fixed cost areas as well as variable ones. With more elements going to fixed costs, total costs are essential.

Variable costs only leave managers in the dilemma of contribution margins. With a variety of products, multiple processes, and trade channels, the contribution margin required with all of these variations to achieve the profit desired can only be determined by knowing the total costs and return on investment with these variations.

Some say that variable costs are an advantage for they are easily understood. This is really an insult to a superior manager. A good manager is certainly capable of understanding variable costs, total costs, and how all these components affect end results.

In fact, one must understand total cost in order to develop the best marketing and business plan. This is essential to move the company into manufacturing processes, products, and markets to concentrate on the strengths of the particular firm and away from the weaknesses of the business relative to competition.

Cash Flow

Cash flow is defined as:

$$\text{Cash Flow} = \text{Depreciation} + \text{Net Profit}.$$

Most cost systems have depreciation in manufacturing cost calculations. This is quite satisfactory. For management decisions, cash flow is an important ingredient, particularly in managing money. Therefore, it is wise to keep depreciation as a separate component on the cost sheet.

Cost sheets should also separate profit into two components, profit retained by the firm and profit paid for taxes. This is absolutely essential in multinational corporations where taxes vary extensively from country to country and from one geographical area to another within a country.

The only thing that is really important to the business manager is net profit. Therefore, this component should be a separate item on the cost sheet so that proper decisions can be rendered.

Operating profit before taxes—and sometimes before interest or other significant charges—is an important guide for certain divisions or segments of the business. It is not the objective of management. The objective of management is profit after tax and cash flow to finance growth. There is nothing to be gained by running a business and risking capital only to pay taxes. Without adequate net returns, the business should either be discontinued or turned over to the particular government for nationalization. Without rewards to the stockholders furnishing the investment or the managers operating the business, operations should be terminated or governments and taxpayers should take the risk and losses.

Net profit must be shown separately on the cost sheets to reflect the actual operating conditions, not theoretical expectations. A firm may have had loss in earlier years and currently have tax credits from this loss. Knowing this fact (not only on the financial statement, but on the cost sheet), managers can make better decisions. This could permit orders to be taken (which might have been refused) to generate a profit and recover this tax gain.

The key to money management (discussed more fully in Chapter Ten) is keeping the interest cost always in front of the management. In Figure 4–1, short-term interest is included as a variable component, whereas long-term financing is shown as a fixed cost.

Material Costs

The initial task is to determine the cost at each step in the cost calculation. This requires detailed costs at process and by cost component.

Where standardized manufacturing components or modules exist, the material cost for an assembled or manufacturing part may be as indicated in Figure 4–2.

The standard prices are the expected prices for the current time interval. Many accountants like to have these set for a year, or at least six months. These rigid time periods cannot be accepted with rapid fluctuations in prices. Standard prices must be updated when a significant change occurs. "Significant" varies with each firm and generally should be an absolute amount which will change the cost a minimum degree. It should not be a percentage. Standard prices can and must be changed within an accounting or fiscal year.

The manager's job is to control operations by using a reliable standard which accurately reflects current conditions. Changing standard prices within an accounting year does not reduce the validity of analysis of variances or financial statements. When time periods for changing standards are too long, managers and accountants tend to hedge for potential raw material price increases. This reduces the validity of costs, budgets, and financial statements for management purposes.

The waste loss is not a historical percentage. It should be calculated based on actual design or engineered standard conditions. These type losses must be updated continually when a specification is changed or tolerance is revised in the manufacturing process.

The waste loss always should be shown as a separate item. As an example, in Figure 4–2 the real material required in Item 1 is $25.00. Since the particular standard sheet size available is 69¼ in. × 47¼ in., a waste loss of 27 percent is generated. By redesign of parts, possibly this loss can be reduced. When real needs and wastes are combined, the waste cost is not highlighted for management attention.

Waste or material losses in factories, as well as permissible off-quality limits, must be engineered based on conditions (by process, product, or other

FIGURE 4–2

Typical Sub-Assembly Bill of Material

Equipment: Washer Units				MATERIAL COSTING				
Sub-Assembly: Rinse Tanks								
Drawing Number: 74–M1001–2				Total Material: $70.15				
Revision Number: Original				Pricing Date: xx/xx/xx				
Date: xx/xx/xx				Priced by: James Jackson				
Sheet: 1 of 1								
Prepared by: James Wilson								

Item	Quantity	Part No.	Description	Total Quantity	Unit	Price	Waste Loss	Total Cost
1	1	Standard	12 Ga.–69¼ in. × 47¼ in. (4.4#)	100#	lb.	$0.25	27	$31.75
2	2	Standard	2 × 2¼ in. (3.2#) × 96 in.	51.2#	lb.	0.25	0	12.80
3	2	Standard	2 × 2¼ in. (3.2#) × 44 in.	11.7#	lb.	0.25	8	3.16
4	2	Standard	1 × 1⅛ in. (.8#) × 44 in.	5.9#	lb.	0.25	8	1.59
5	2	Standard	1 × 1⅛ in. (.8#) × 46 in.	6.1#	lb.	0.25	4	1.59
6	2	Standard	1 × 1⅛ in. (.8#) × 11 in.	1.5#	lb.	0.25	4	.39
7	1	Standard	1 × 1⅛ in. (.8#) × 65½ in.	4.4#	lb.	0.25	18	1.30
8	4	3–31–0707	2 in. × 6 in. Piano Hinge	2 ft.	ft.	1.00	0	2.00
9	2	4–16–3727	Louver Panel	2	Ea.	3.91	0	7.82
			Miscellaneous Pipe Fittings					1.75
			Hardware, Welding Rod					1.50
			Paint, etc.					4.50
			Total Module Cost					$70.15

significant difference). *These losses must never be accounted for in cost by averages, history, or other unidentifiable cost basis.*

COST AT PROCESS

The cost at each production, assembly, or other process must be precise. These must reflect the variables affecting the cost—lot size, production speed, or other situations unique to a particular product or stockkeeping item.

A summary for a process cost involving final assembly, painting, and drying on a production line basis is indicated in Figure 4–3. Complete details of cost calculation can be obtained from other references.[2]

Personnel cost can be summarized from the labor complement and expected hourly rates as displayed in Figure 4–4. These must include potential increases. They must be developed specifically from individual job titles and specific rates.

The actual determination of standard cost by stockkeeping item, process, or other element is a responsibility of a professional industrial engineering department. In general, industrial engineers should set standards for all variable production parameters—personnel, waste, or material loss. (Department titles, such as "Methods and Standards Departments," should be discarded.)

---

[2] Wilson, *Industrial Cost Controls.*

FIGURE 4–3

Final Assembly, Painting, and Drying Process

Item	Cost per Year	Cost per Week 48 Week/Year	Cost per Hour 72 Hours/Week
Personnel......................	$192,000	$ 4,000	$ 55.56
Fuel and supplies.................	72,000	1,500	20.83
Variable expenses.................	48,000	1,000	13.89
Fixed expenses...................	84,000	1,750	24.31
Depreciation.....................	144,000	3,000	41.66
Totals...................	$540,000	$11,250	$156.25

FIGURE 4–4

Hourly Personnel Complement—Process A

Job Title	Shift Complement 1st	2d	Rate per Hour	Each $/Week	Total $/Week
Job No. 1......................	1	1	$6.00	$240	$ 480
Job No. 2......................	1	1	$5.00	$200	$ 400
Job No. 3......................	1	1	$4.00	$160	$ 320
Job No. 4......................	2	2	$3.50	$140	$ 560
Job No. 5......................	1	1	$3.25	$130	$ 260
Totals...................	6	6			$2,020

Fuel and supply costs must be calculated based on known conditions and expenses. An example of the cost calculation for gas is shown in Figure 4–5. Plant and mechanical engineers know these factors. They should be utilized in cost calculations.

The cost should reflect expected rate increases. The gas cost should not be based on a historical average cost per week or per hour. It must be defined based on engineering requirements for BTUs per hour, quality of the gas, and running hours. In this case, the cost per 72 running hours is $648, or $31,104 per 48-week year.

Engineered calculations are extremely important on new equipment. A new dryer may be installed with engineered specifications to consume ten million BTUs of gas at a given production rate. When it is in production, operations must be compared to these engineering performance standards. It is possible that suppliers may not have properly installed a piece of equipment. It may be that losses are occurring or inefficient devices are being utilized to obtain the maximum heat conversion. Only by comparing actual

FIGURE 4–5

Calculation of Gas Cost
(assembly, painting, and drying)

Description	Drying
BTUs/hour	9,270,000
BTU content—1.03*	1,030
Cubic feet/hour	9,000
Hours/week	80
Run time	90%
Running hours/week	72
Cubic feet/week	648,000
1,000 cubic feet/week	648
Cost/1,000 cu. feet†	$ 1.00
Cost/week	$ 648.00
Cost/year—48 weeks	$31,104.00

* 1,030 BTUs/cubic feet.
† Rates vary drastically between types or supply, volumes of usage, rate adjustments, and geographical areas.

operations against calculated or engineered performance bases can design, construction, or operating losses be discovered or potential cost savings be located. Heat recovery units could be installed to cut these costs in the short term.

The normal volume in this example is two eight-hour shifts per day for 48 weeks each year. This allows four weeks of down time each year for holidays, vacations, and other factors. The number of weeks operation and shifts per day is extremely important. It varies extensively by industry and country from continuous operations to reduced operations of one shift or even less.

In many countries, as a result of continuing increases in vacations, holidays, and other benefits, the operating weeks per year have dropped to 45 or less. This has reduced productivity of both personnel and assets to the point where some industries in some countries are not competitive in the world market.

Return on capital employed is achieved by operating capital intensified equipment to the maximum extent, given personnel, social, and maintenance limitations. Continuous operation does not necessarily imply continuous working by people. It can be achieved by rotating shifts, rotating days, or other acceptable alternatives.

Every cost element—whether gas, supplies, social benefits, or other variable expenses—must be calculated based on known conditions. Historical averages, percentages, and allocations must be completely eliminated. This applies to maintenance and other service cost centers as well as to the productive processes.

In Figure 4–3, the depreciation cost is $144,000 per year. Dividing this sum by 48 weeks per year, the cost per week is $3,000. Using 72 operating hours per week, the cost per hour is $3,000 divided by 72, or $41.66 per hour.

With inflation, radical changes in prices of equipment, and fluctuating currency values, depreciation for costing and pricing purposes should generally be on replacement value. It is absolutely essential that management recover in the marketplace sufficient funds to replace its buildings and equipment in present value monetary units. This does not cause any accounting or taxation difficulties. It does create a difference between cost depreciation and accounting depreciation for income tax statements. This can be handled as a variance without disrupting cost calculations for pricing, inventory evaluation, or tax accounting.

By using replacement values, the assumption is made that the business intends to stay in existence within the life of the asset. Where an industry has a product or facility which is in the declining portion of the life cycle and replacement is not expected, depreciation should be completely eliminated from the cost calculation for pricing to extend the life cycle of the asset of product even if book value exists. Managers must determine the logic and approach to the business. Then, the policy relative to the asset depreciation calculations, cost calculations, inventory evaluations, pricing, and taxation must be specified. Taxation aspects are a special problem requiring more in-depth study than is contained in these pages.

Theoretical discussions on replacement value versus book value are important only in influencing management to make the proper logical decision relative to the business strategy. In addition to the value utilized, the life of the asset is the next most important factor for management consideration. Asset lives may be influenced by wearout expectations of the equipment, tax rules, technology, or styling. In every case, the life utilized for cost and pricing purposes should be the most realistic one. The wearout life of a particular piece of equipment may be 20 years. Tax laws may allow a period of 15 years. The technology, styling, or cost competitiveness may reduce the useful life to ten years. In this situation, ten years should be used for cost calculations and pricing decisions. This change, like replacement versus book value, does not disrupt general accounting or taxation. It can be handled in a variance account with little practical difficulty.

Wherever the machine is the primary unit, all costs must be on a machine hour basis. In many cases, even where personnel cost is most significant, the costs are still more valid on a machine hour basis. The calculation of cost for variable or fixed expenses based on a percentage of personnel costs, percentage or ratio of material costs, and other relationships which vary by product or stockkeeping item is highly suspect.

The cost for fuel in most production processes has no relationship to personnel or labor costs. It is related to maintenance of heat required for a given level of production. Supply cost is a factor of machine hours operated, production quantity and other technical factors. These and other components of cost may have no relationship to the cost of material being processed or personnel utilized. Every cost must be calculated and applied to the cost sheet based on the cause, the reason. These may be by machine hour, unit produced, or other basis. Rarely is a percentage, ratio, or other type of markup correct or right.

Managers will often employ expensive personnel for research, manufacturing, and other functions. Then, cost calculations are simplified to the point where they are meaningless. Professional managers must insist that cost calculations precisely reflect costs based on cause and conditions. There is no reason to use a very expensive automated lathe to produce a part without knowing the cost. There is no reason to use a high priced computer installation to compile inaccurate information.

Cost by Lot Size

After costs and expenses by process, account, machine hour, or other basis are determined, costs based on production or other conditions must be determined. Using data contained in Figure 4–3, an example of cost by lot size and changeover time for final assembly, painting, and drying is listed in Figure 4–6.

Here, products are divided into two categories based on production variables. Category I products deliver 50 units per hour and require 30 minutes changeover time. Category II products deliver 25 units per hour and require 120 minutes of changeover time.

Under Category I for Product Number 1492, a lot size of 100 units requires 2.00 hours of process time and 0.50 hours (30 minutes) of changeover time for a total of 2.50 hours. The cost per run can be obtained by multiplying the 2.50 hours times the personnel cost per hour or $55.56 for a total cost per run of personnel of $138.90. For a 100-unit production run, the cost, then, is $1.39 per unit. The cost for a lot size of 1,000 is reduced to $1.14 per unit.

Given the conditions listed, costs per unit vary extensively. No doubt, the market and competition does influence the final selling price. Yet, knowing the real cost, managers can select from the market those items which will give the best financial results. Certainly, in bidding on contract, large private label purchases, or other special pricing opportunities, cost per unit run is important.

Even if market prices must be the determining factor, by knowing the true cost based on cause, managers can more adequately control cost, optimize production, and inventory control. Where management science techniques of linear programming and economic order quantities are employed (either with automatic data processing or manual methods), the results obtained from these mathematical techniques are no better than the cost data made available.

Managers must insist that costs are correct. They must understand the basis and details to insure that errors have not been made in calculations.

FIGURE 4–6

Cost Calculation by Lot Size and Changeover Time

Product Number	Lot Size	Hours				Cost					
		Process Time	Change-over Time	Total Time		Personnel	Fuel and Supplies	Variable Expenses	Fixed Expenses	Depreciation	Total
Category I: 50 Units per Hour and 30 Minutes Changeover Time											
1492.........	100	2.00	0.50	2.50	Cost per run	$ 138.90	$ 52.08	$ 34.73	$ 60.78	$ 104.15	$ 390.63
					Cost per unit	1.39	0.52	0.35	0.61	1.04	3.91
2199.........	1,000	20.00	0.50	20.50	Cost per run	$1,138.98	$427.02	$284.75	$498.36	$854.03	$3,203.03
					Cost per unit	1.14	0.43	0.28	0.50	0.85	3.20
Category II: 25 Units per Hour and 120 Minutes Changeover Time											
2121.........	50	2.00	2.00	4.00	Cost per run	$ 222.24	$ 83.32	$ 55.56	$ 97.24	$ 166.64	$ 625.00
					Cost per unit	4.44	1.67	1.11	1.94	3.33	12.50
4821.........	1,000	40.00	2.00	42.00	Cost per run	$2,333.52	$874.86	$583.38	$1,021.02	$1,749.72	$6,562.50
					Cost per unit	2.33	0.87	0.58	1.02	1.75	6.56

Then, managers must use this information! Sometimes, managers tend to let logic be the determining factor for a decision. This "shooting from the hip" type of decision must be replaced by decisions based on analytical and objective information.

DISTRIBUTION, SELLING, MERCHANDISING, AND ADMINISTRATIVE EXPENSES

The same attention should be given to the determination and calculation of distribution, selling, merchandising, and administrative expenses as is given to manufacturing cost. Detailed manufacturing expenses are sometimes determined; then, a broad brush approach is taken to these other expenses.

A listing of nonmanufacturing expenses is contained in Figure 4–7. The chart of accounts must be sufficiently precise so that expenses can be assigned directly to the responsible executive. With the proper definition, very few expenses need be "allocated" or "distributed." The same engineered approach must be taken to these costs and expenses by the accounting staff as the Industrial Engineering Department would use to specify manufacturing cost. It is interesting to note from Figure 4–7 that practically all expenses are "direct." Very few are distributed or allocated. As an example, fixed social security costs can be determined by calculation from the salary personnel complement by the specific area of responsibility.

For inventory pricing, as well as marketing needs, it is important to determine what a manufacturing expense is, and what it is not. A machinery manufacturer may have field service costs for equipment at outlying locations. A portion of this may be installation cost, which is easily definable. Other field service costs could be for maintenance and repair during the warranty of the equipment. A part of this expense may be associated with nonwarranty requirements as a service to a customer or to generate sales. That portion of the cost associated with manufacturing and warranty is a manufacturing expense for placing a first quality piece of equipment into normal operations. Field service costs and expense associated with customer service for other marketing reasons or to generate sales of products would be a selling expense.

The key to determining expense of this type is asking the question, "What is our business?"[3] If it is equipment manufacturing, then it is an equipment manufacturing expense. If the primary business is selling a product (as an example, chemicals utilized in the equipment), then the expense is one of selling. It is important to properly segment these costs where equipment may be both leased or sold. Unless they are properly accounted for, equipment which is sold may be overcosted and thereby reduce an important opportunity for growth; whereas equipment which is leased may be undercosted.

In further analyzing field service costs for equipment, it is important to note that these costs are not influenced by percentage of sales. It takes a

---

[3] Theodore Levitt, *Innovations in Marketing* (New York: McGraw-Hill Book Company, 1962), p. 76.

FIGURE 4–7

Summary of Sales, Merchandising, Administration, and Distribution Expenses
(in thousands of dollars)

Account	Distribution	Sales	Merchandising and Product Planning	Administration	Total	Basis for Distribution
Salaries and bonus	$ 310	$1,085	$230	$ 360	$1,985	Direct
Travel expense	5	220	20	25	270	Direct
Insurance—property	—	—	—	10	10	Direct
Taxes—property	35	5	—	5	45	Direct
Insurance—inventory	10	—	—	—	10	Distribution
Taxes—inventory	75	—	—	—	75	Distribution
Depreciation	80	10	45	20	155	Direct
Salary continuation and pension	30	40	15	65	150	Direct
Fixed social security	20	30	10	35	95	Direct
Hospital and group insurance	10	20	5	25	60	Direct
Employee education and training	5	10	5	15	35	Direct
Office maintenance and repair	5	—	5	10	15	Direct
Electric power	10	—	10	15	35	Office sq. ft.
Workmen's compensation	5	5	—	10	20	Direct
Unemployment compensation	5	5	—	15	25	Direct
Data processing rent, supplies and salaries	200	50	—	100	350	Computer hrs.
Legal fees	—	—	—	20	20	Direct
Professional services	5	15	5	15	40	Direct
Auditors	—	—	—	40	40	Direct
Association fees	5	10	5	20	40	Direct
Dues and subscriptions	—	5	—	10	15	Salary employees
Office equipment rent	—	—	—	15	15	Direct
Postage	15	35	—	25	75	Direct
Telephone and telegraph	120	40	—	40	200	Direct
Office supplies	10	70	—	20	100	Direct
Advertising	—	560	—	—	560	Direct
Donations	—	—	—	25	25	Direct
Materials and supplies	—	—	75	—	75	Direct
Branch offices	—	150	—	—	150	Direct
Sample expense (net)	—	550	—	—	550	Direct
Warehouse expense and freight (net)	600	—	—	—	600	Direct
Corporate administration	—	—	—	230	230	Direct
Total	$1,560	$2,915	$425	$1,170	$6,070	
Variable	560	765	0	0		
Fixed	1,000	2,150	425	1,170		

field service person as long to reach the site to service a $1,000 item of equipment as it does to service a $10,000 item of equipment. In these cases, field service costs must be properly isolated between those costs which are caused by a per unit, and those caused by the technology or operating conditions of the equipment.

Data processing expenses are an excellent example of money which can either be used effectively and efficiently or wasted. The expenses for this department must be assigned to the various executive responsibilities based on computer hours for operating cost. For new projects, systems and procedures expenses should be approved utilizing a format procedure similar to capital expenditures. The system's costs must be estimated for a new system and then charges assigned to that project. This brings cost discipline to new projects as well as the cost per machine or assembly line hour. A weekly cost control report (see Chapter Five) should be produced on computer operations as well as on manufacturing processes.

Once the costs by executive responsibility have been listed, these must be separated by trade channel as shown in Figure 4–8.

Practically all salaries and travel expenses of sales personnel can be directly assigned to the various trade channels—retail, wholesale, large volume, or other channels of distribution. Some top level salaries must be assigned. Even in these cases, there is generally a basis—the number of salesmen supervised, the time required by the executive for a specific area, or other factors.

Even in selling many expenses are direct. Telephone charges are a good example of a direct expense. Data processing costs can be separated. Postage and similar expenses can be sorted out based on actual conditions of actual mailings. In all cases, it is not necessary that every dollar be accounted for in the expense accumulation by trade channel. It is important that 75 to 85 percent of the expenses be assignable specifically.

In the customer service area, it requires the same amount of time in communication expenses to receive, enter, and process an order for one gallon of paint as it does 100 cases of paint. A complexity factor or distribution of these expenses must separate the cause of these costs by product category, customer type, distribution channel, or other meaningful basis.

Normally, any distribution of expenses based on percentage of sales is highly questionable. In these situations, those areas generating the highest sales volume carry the highest costs, whereas those with the lowest sales volume create the most costs.

Some administrative personnel seem to indicate that if all expenses cannot be accounted for exactly, there is no need for detailing sales, distribution, merchandising, research, or administrative costs. *This is untrue!* The assignment of costs in detail is necessary to that extent whereby a significant error would not be made in a product cost.

In Figure 4–8, some advertising and sample expenses are assigned to "Private Label." Some private label, mail order, and other large volume pur-

FIGURE 4–8

Selling Expenses
(in thousands of dollars)

Account	Private Label	Wholesale	Retail	Total	Basis for Distribution
Salaries and bonus................	$270	$315	$ 500	$1,085	Direct
Travel expense....................	60	60	100	220	Direct
Taxes—property..................	2	1	2	5	Sales
Depreciation.....................	3	3	4	10	Direct
Salary continuation and pension.....	5	5	10	20	Direct
Fixed social security..............	10	10	15	35	Direct
Hospital and group insurance........	5	10	10	25	Direct
Employee education and training.....	5	5	10	20	Direct
Workmen's compensation...........	1	2	3	6	Direct
Unemployment compensation........	1	1	2	4	Direct
Data processing rent and supplies....	9	33	8	50	Direct
Professional services..............	5	5	5	15	Direct
Association fees...................	3	3	3	9	Direct
Dues and subscriptions.............	2	2	2	6	Direct
Postage.........................				[35	Complexity
Telephone and telegraph............	25	95	25	[40	Complexity
Office supplies...................				[70	Complexity
Advertising......................	100	195	265	560	Estimate
Branch offices....................	—	60	90	150	Direct
Sample expense (net)..............	150	80	320	550	Direct
Total.....................	$656	$885	$1,374	$2,915	
Variable....................	$195	$220	$ 350	$ 765	
Fixed.....................	$461	$665	$1,024	$2,150	
				$2,915	

chasers would have suppliers believe that research and development, advertising and promotion expenses are not applicable to their sales. Some firms have believed that these expenses are based on retail or wholesale requirements. Then, large volume and private label sales need not be assigned any of these costs. In many cases, this is incorrect. It has resulted in private label, mail order, or other large volume sales being taken at too low a price. This practice has permitted a swing from retail and wholesale to the larger volume purchases. In addition to being incorrect, it has permitted these larger volume purchasers to take a greater control of certain product distributions. It has caused the decline of regular retail and wholesale business. Further, it has caused some manufacturers to be squeezed between their raw material suppliers and customers. This loss of business control reduces the potential financial results.

It is true that retail sales with a large number of accounts and lower sales dollars per order do have an added cost. Yet, these can be determined and assigned.

A listing of distribution, sales, merchandising, and administrative expenses by channel of distribution for conversion to cost sheet calculations is contained in Figure 4–9.

In this example, the distribution cost for the retail channel of distribution is $0.200; whereas, for private label, it is $0.075. The order entry costs are higher, for more people are required to handle orders. Other expenses vary accordingly. Many items are related to units, not to a percentage of cost. Distribution, merchandising, and administration are all placed on a unit basis.

Sales are on a percentage markup. In some cases, these functions must be separated with a certain portion or certain accounts on units and some on percentage or ratio markup.

For this particular example, the sales expense markup of retail and wholesale is combined. This reflects an organizational situation where regional salesmen have both retail and wholesale accounts. In general, where the sales force is separated, the cost of selling to wholesalers would be lower than retail. Even in a case where the sales individual handles retail and wholesale

FIGURE 4–9

Calculations for Conversion to Cost Sheet

	Amount	÷	Units	=	Dollars per Unit
Distribution expense markup					
Private label	$ 140,000		5,200,000		.027 Var./unit
	250,000		5,200,000		.048 Fixed/unit
	390,000		5,200,000		.075 Total/unit
Retail	215,000		3,000,000		.072 Var./unit
	385,000		3,000,000		.128 Fixed/unit
	600,000		3,000,000		.200 Total/unit
Wholesale	205,000		4,800,000		.043 Var./unit
	365,000		4,800,000		.076 Fixed/unit
	$ 570,000		4,800,000		.119 Total/unit

	Amount	÷	Mfg. Cost (first quality)	=	Multiplier × First Quality Mfg. Cost
Sales expense markup					
Private label	$ 195,000		$14,000,000		.014 Variable
	461,000		14,000,000		.033 Fixed
	656,000		14,000,000		.047 Total
Retail and wholesale	570,000		$21,150,000		.027 Variable
	1,689,000		21,150,000		.080 Fixed
	$2,259,000		21,150,000		.107 Total

	Amount	÷	Units	=	Dollars per Unit
Merchandising and product planning					
All sales	$ 425,000		13,000,000		.033 Fixed/unit
Administration					
Private label	$ 380,000		5,200,000		.073 Fixed/unit
Retail	440,000		3,000,000		.147 Fixed/unit
Wholesale	350,000		4,800,000		.073 Fixed/unit

accounts combined, it would be wise to study this sales cost in depth and, where necessary, subdivide the selling cost between retail and wholesale. This is particularly important where sales incentives and commissions are a sizeable portion of the selling expense.

Utilization of percentages for administrative and any other expenses is wrong. In practically every case, percentage application overstates the total cost of higher priced products and understates the cost of lower priced products. This situation has led many businesses into selling lower priced merchandise. It has led to reduced sales of medium and higher priced items.

A characteristic of superior managers is that they know and understand their costs—material costs, variable costs, fixed costs, and others. They know how to use these data to improve their pricing, distribution, and competitive strategy in both short-term and long-range situations.

Managers should:

Review the existing cost calculation methods. Where necessary, managers should insist that corrections and improvements be implemented.

Check to see that costs submitted are timely and reflect current conditions rather than a particular budget year or other time period.

Revise the cost information to obtain multiple guides to business management—gross margin, value added, contribution margin, cash flow, and profit.

Follow up to insure that fixed costs are studied, refined, and calculated precisely.

Review the separation of cost components by trade channel and area of responsibility to place them in the proper place by cause of cost.

Discontinue the utilization of percentages, ratios, and other easy techniques of cost calculation.

Staff the Cost Accounting Department with professional people capable of taking an engineered approach to all expenses.

Superior managers understand costs and financial information, and how one decision relates to another in the total business.

There is no need to operate a business on only one theory—contribution accounting, full absorption costing, or other basis. Managers need to know or have available every guide possible which can influence business decisions —gross margins, value added, contribution margin, cash flow, and profit.

Incorrect or misleading terminology, such as overhead, indirect labor, and others should be eliminated. Correct terminology should be used. When words are devalued, people and ideas are devalued.[4]

---

[4] Edwin Newman, *Strictly Speaking* (Indianapolis: The Bobbs-Merrill Co., Inc., 1974), p. 5.

The utilization of percentages, ratios, and other easy techniques must be eliminated. In general, percentage markups overprice higher priced products and underprice lower cost ones.

Costs must be calculated by cause with the same precision as engineered standards are set in the factory. Averages must be eliminated and replaced with calculated costs. Wherever a significant variation occurs by lot size, condition, or other parameter, costs must be separated to reflect these causes and conditions.

Distribution, sales, merchandising, and administrative expenses are excellent opportunities to improve the determination of costs, both for pricing and control. Little distribution or allocation of these expenses is necessary when accounts are properly defined and segregated.

It is true that the market may frequently determine the selling price. Yet, by knowing true costs, managers can select from the market those items, those channels of distribution, and those customers which will generate the most profit, and provide the best short-term financial results within the constraints of the firm, the market, and the technology.

In the short term and for businesses in crises, managers must insure that cost calculations are correct in order to make the right decisions for cost reduction and pricing. In many businesses in trouble, the reason can be traced to faulty cost calculations, excessive safety built into calculations by accountants, and erroneous presentation of information to management.

chapter *FIVE*

Engineered Expense Control

*Cost control is not an isolated function or
department. It is a philosophy, a way of life for
every person—from the executive suite to the
factory floor—in the cost effective firm.*

Foundation for Planned Systematic Management

FOCUS ON MANUFACTURING, maintain a low cost and high volume operation; then, manufacturing production operations will become a competitive edge in the market.

Control of expenses starts with management information reports comparing actual results with standard operations based on engineered conditions.

A complete management information system will include control reports at the following levels:

1. Top management.
2. Plant or equivalent management.
3. Department or shift supervisor.
4. Individual control reports for selected items or expenses.

A typical top management report may be as indicated in Figure 5–1, "Management Overview of Financial Results."

TOP MANAGEMENT

Any good report has three views—a look at the past, a look at the present, and a look at the future. It is always necessary for managers to know where they have been, where they are, and where they are going. In addition to statistics for the current month and year-to-date, the forecast should be included based on the best estimate at that point.

Too often, management control reports and financial statements are too complex. The real need is to present to management a report from which they can ask questions—the right questions, the true and important questions, (Chapter One). It is not necessary to have extensive and detailed reports which answer all questions that might arise. These are answered with follow-up special studies or additional analyses.

A key part of this report is the comparison of actual results to the plan. The term "budget" is sometimes used. This is misleading. By definition, a budget is a plan of systematic spending. Likewise, by definition, a plan is a way of proceeding. *This is what management is all about—developing a way of proceeding.*

73

FIGURE 5–1

Management Overview of Financial Results

Month Ending _____
Date Issued _____

	Current Month				Year-to-Date				Forecast—Year			
	Plan	This Year	Last Year	Base Year	Plan	This Year	Last Year	Base Year	Plan	This Year	Last Year	Base Year
Units sold												
Gross sales												
Less discounts and terms												
Net sales												
Materials												
Gross Margin												
Purchases												
Value Added												
Variable cost												
Contribution												
Fixed cost												
Depreciation												
Taxes												
Net Profit												
Cash flow												
Variances												
Materials												
Purchases												
Variable cost												
Fixed cost												
Profit												
Cash flow												

The management reports should be in a format similar to that for the Cost Sheet Summary (Chapter Four, Figure 4–1). In this way, management can relate its control statements to the cost information made available to them.

In this statement, there are no percentages. Superior managers develop a plan and proceed to find a way of achieving that plan. The need is to obtain the best financial results in absolute amounts, not in some arbitrary percentage.

Percentage of sales and other similar guides are easy and helpful. Business reports sometimes include the statement, "Profits up 123 percent." A more thorough reading of the fine print indicates that 123 percent of nothing is still nothing. The real need is for management to set absolute targets and strive to achieve these goals. Even though percentage of sales, contribution percentage, and other bases may be interesting and helpful, they should be eliminated from the business reports. This will force management to concentrate attention on the need to compare absolute results with absolute objectives.

Any good management control report includes variances to explain why the objective or planned profit was or was not achieved. A summary statement of this type should include only total categories of variances. Then, meaningful, more detailed reports can be brought to management's attention.

Another key column of information in Figure 5–1 is "Base Year." As an example, the Base Year could be two, three, or more years earlier. Then, the data for the Base Year is "indexed" or "ratioed" to adjust for inflation and monetary value changes. This permits management to evaluate its current performance in real terms against the preceding "Base Year" data. Where inflation is running in two digits or important changes take place in monetary values, it is necessary to "index" the financial results for the "Last Year." Indexing is the application of adjustments to data that places them on a constant basis.

Many managers are deluding themselves by thinking that inflationary gains are real improvements in performance. Firms with international branches can be misled in a similar way when currency values change. Professional managers must insist that data which represent real financial results over the time period be made available systematically.

Indexing is not only necessary in inflationary times, it is helpful in deflationary periods and in countries where currency values are strengthening. However, based on the past few decades of economic experience, indexing for deflationary periods seems highly theoretical. Currency values are more a function of balance of payments and foreign exchange position relative to another currency. These may be independent of domestic inflation or deflation. Cases of any currency increasing general domestic purchasing power are rare. A decline of prices of a particular product is usually caused by competition, new processes, supply and demand relationships, or other factors, rather than deflation.

It is, of course, impossible at this time to utilize "indexing" methods for tax reporting. For internal management purposes, statements must be prepared to properly reflect true performance. This requires adjustments at the year end for tax or public reporting purposes.

DEPARTMENTAL LEVEL REPORTING

A report for a plant or similar operating unit may be as indicated in Figure 5–2. Here, too, the breakout of control remains on the key components—materials, purchases, variable costs, and fixed costs. This is a similar format to that of the cost sheet summary.

The manufacturing value added is:

Manufacturing Value Added = Total Cost — Materials — Purchases

This is necessary for those managers who utilize the value added concept. In addition, it is needed to tie into the cost sheet and make available input data and variance analysis for management control reports.

A typical Department Cost Control Report for a Data Processing Department is presented in Figure 5–3. It is important that cost control reports be prepared for Service and Administrative Departments as well as for manufacturing units. Data processing, like production units, is adding value through a service which can be recovered in the market; otherwise, large expenses for data processing installations should be discouraged. The computer or business machine should be evaluated and controlled as any piece of production equipment.

Previously, cost calculations were placed on a machine hour or process hour basis. Large, centralized data processing departments should be on a cost per minute or even a cost per second basis. As an example, consider a data processing expense of $480,000 per year including systems, procedures, and all related management and administrative expenses. The operations may be on a 48-week per year normal time and netting 80 productive hours per week. The costs are:

Cost per year	$480,000.00
Cost per week—48 weeks	10,000.00
Cost per hour—80 hours/week	125.00
Cost per minute	2.08
Cost per second	0.035

Here, the cost per minute is $2.08 and the cost per second is $0.035 for every minute and every second of an 80-hour week for 48 weeks per year. This is a true expense which must be controlled in detail and effectively utilized.

The reports contained in Figures 5–2 and 5–3 are on biweekly time intervals. To tie in to quarterly statements, seven reports are required during the 13-week quarter. In most cases, a weekly personnel cost control report is needed. Larger, more labor intensified industries require personnel cost reports on a daily or even a shift basis. These reports are not intended to replace on-the-spot, timely process or production checks to monitor periodically or continuously important aspects of the operations.

FIGURE 5-2

Cost Control Report

Department _____ W/E _____	This 2 Weeks			Last 13 Weeks		
	Standard $	Actual $	Variance $	Standard $	Actual $	Variance $
Materials						
Material A						
Material B						
Material C						
Material D						
Packing						
Subtotal: materials						
Purchases						
Supplies						
Repairs						
Utilities						
Fuels						
Subtotal: purchases						
Variable cost						
Personnel						
In-process loss						
Waste						
Personnel benefits						
Subtotal: variable cost						
Fixed cost						
Salaries						
Depreciation						
Insurance						
Property tax						
Personnel benefits						
Subtotal: fixed cost						
Total cost						
Value added						

FIGURE 5–3

Data Processing Controllable Cost Statement

Cost Item	This Week			Last 13 Weeks		
	Standard $	Actual $	Variance $	Standard $	Actual $	Variance $
Personnel						
Input control personnel						
Computer operators						
Auxiliary equipment operators						
Output control personnel						
Clerical personnel						
Subtotal: personnel						
Variable						
Cards and input supplies						
Paper and output supplies						
Other supplies						
Electricity and utilities						
Subtotal: variable						
Fixed cost						
Equipment rental						
Equipment maintenance						
Salaries						
Office rental						
Subtotal: fixed cost						
Total						

FIGURE 5–3 (continued)

Cost Item	This Week			Last 13 Weeks		
	Standard $	Actual $	Variance $	Standard $	Actual $	Variance $
Key ratios						
Operating cost per hour						
Operating hours						
Downtime hours testing						
Downtime hours other						
Total hours						
Efficiency						
Number of employees						
Input errors reported						
Output errors reported						
Total						

It is necessary for all the costs under a particular supervisor or manager's responsibility to be brought together on one page. A personnel report may be received from one department, a material control report from another, and variable or fixed cost expenses from another. These need to be combined and coordinated so that the responsible person can see his total performance.

The reporting period—one week, two weeks, or monthly—is determined by the dynamics of the operation. Where control can be quickly lost, more frequent reports are required. When reports are issued too frequently, they do not receive supervisory attention. When they are prepared too infrequently, conditions may change within that time interval and cause the report to be useless for action.

MATERIAL CONTROL

In Figure 5–2, materials are summarized for a particular process, department, or cost center. The more detailed statement by these segments is required as exhibited in Figure 5–4.

This report includes units and dollars. The good material report must include units and values. In some cases, a large loss in units may be a very trivial loss in value. In others, a very small loss in units with a high value can result in excessive financial differences.

Many firms use the term "waste" for material left from production

FIGURE 5–4

Weekly Material Control Report

Plant _____
Week Ended _____
Two Weeks Ending
Cumulative: _____
Weeks-to-Date

	Actual Units	Standard Units	Variance Units (Over) Under	Actual $	Standard $	Variance $ (Over) Under	Dept. Responsible	Variance $ (Over) Under
PROCESS A Material A								
Material B								
Material C								
Material D								
Material E								
Subtotal: Process A								
PROCESS B Material 1								
Material 2								
Material 3								
Material 4								
Material 5								
Subtotal: Process B								
PROCESS C Material A								
Material B								
Material C								
Material D								
Material E								
Subtotal: Process C								
PROCESS D Material A								
Material B								
Material C								
Material D								
Subtotal: Process D								
Grand total								

processes. This antique term should be eliminated. It implies that materials lost are of little value. The improvement in yield from raw material to finished product is a meaningful way to improve short-term financial results.

The materials which should be lost must be determined on an engineered basis. These should be specified with "specification sheets" developed to give standard definitions, descriptions of material, department reporting, method of calculation, and responsibility. An example is contained in Figure 5–5.

FIGURE 5–5
Material Loss Specification Sheet

	SEAMS
	Standard
	$1.00
	$ Loss per POUND

STANDARD:	Seams
DESCRIPTION:	Seams cut at inspection to square rolls
DEPARTMENT REPORTING:	Inspection
DEPARTMENT RESPONSIBLE:	All departments who cut or sew seams
MATERIAL INVOLVED:	Finished goods
COLLECTION POINT:	Inspection station
BASIS FOR STANDARD:	
Selected Size of Cut:	12" × 72"
Frequency of Standard:	One cut per roll, inspected
DERIVATION OF STANDARD:	Standards vary by category of material, by weight ranges. These ranges are as below:

Finished Goods Weight/Linear Yd.	Pounds/Seam
1.00–1.50 = 1.25 lb.	0.42
1.50–2.00 = 1.75 lb.	0.58
2.00–2.50 = 2.25 lb.	0.75
2.50–3.00 = 2.75 lb.	0.92
3.00–3.50 = 3.25 lb.	1.08
3.50–4.00 = 3.75 lb.	1.25
4.00–4.50 = 4.25 lb.	1.42
4.50–5.00 = 4.75 lb.	1.55

CALCULATION OF STANDARD: The total standard allowed pounds per week is calculated by multiplying the pounds per seam by weight range multiplied by the number of rolls finished.

This one is for typical cloth lost in a textile, apparel, rubber coating, or other process utilizing cloth, sheets, or similar materials. The development of material lost standards, either by the Industrial Engineering Department or the Quality Control Department, is an excellent way to reduce excessive losses and maintain control.

IN-PROCESS YIELD

In-process yield is the relationship of packed finished products to the raw materials placed into the initial production process. As an example, should 1,000 gear blanks be placed into the machine shop and 960 gears be completed for finished goods, the yield would be:

$$\text{Yield} = \frac{960}{1,000} \times 100 = 96.0\%$$

A typical in-process yield report is presented in Figure 5–6.

Reports of this type can be prepared based on the manufacturing process —batches, rolls, manufacturing order, or other unit of measure. They must always include units loss and dollar value. These reports can be utilized to improve process control. They are necessary for manufacturing accounting to write down inventory losses.

Losses may be occurring due to conversion in the manufacturing process, theft, inaccurate reporting, or other reasons.

In-process yield reports can be subtotaled by product category, product type, or other meaningful basis.

An off-quality report to supplement the in-process yield reports may be as featured in Figure 5–7. It is important to separate in-process loss—whether caused by personnel or machine performance—from off-quality. Where particular products have high off-quality or reject amounts, the engineering specifications might be reviewed for potential change. The machine could be checked for control or tool replacement. Incoming materials must always be cleared by receiving quality control. Rejections must be included on off-quality reports and transmitted to accounting to insure that these raw material invoices are not paid, that deductions are made for off-quality raw materials, and claims recovered from suppliers.

Factory reports must be verified to insure credibility. In some situations, manufacturing reports indicate off-quality or in-process to be a small percentage or even an improving trend when this is not really the case. Any control report from any department must be verified from a separate source to insure correctness. This separate source is normally the accounting department's statements comparing reported losses in manufacturing to actual losses in inventories, invoices, or other documentation.

ANALYSIS OF VARIANCE

In addition to the in-process loss control of materials, an analysis of variance of materials is required for management. A Material Control Statement is presented in Figure 5–8.

FIGURE 5-6

In-Process Yield Report

Week Ending: _____

(1) Batch No.	(2) Description	(3) Part No.	(4) Size Gear Blanks	(5) Blanks Machined	(6) Gears Finished	(7) Gears Inspected	(8) Lost Blanks to Inspection (Explanation)	(9) Units	(10) $ Each	(11) $ Total
									Total Lost	
10211	Gear 6 in. Standard	9103-2	750	745	740	738	In-Process Loss	12	$10	$120

FIGURE 5-7

Off-Quality and In-Process Yield Report

Batch No.	Description	Part No.	Gear Blanks Finished	Source of Off-quality						Total Finished Gears First Quality	Description of Off-quality	Total Lost				
				Supplier	Machine Process 1	Machine Process 2	Machine Process 3	Final Inspection				Total Off-quality	Reclaimed from Suppliers	Net Off-quality	Loss Each	Total
10211	Gear 6 in. standard	9103-2	738	7	3	0	3	5		720	Failure to meet design tolerances	18	7	11	$15.00*	$165.00

* = Raw material cost plus manufacturing loss.

FIGURE 5-8

Material Control Statement

Department Material—Unit	Units (00)			Dollars (00)			Analysis of Gain (Loss) ($000)				
	Standard Usage	Actual Usage	Gain (Loss)	Standard Usage	Actual Usage Standard $	Actual Usage Actual $	Yield	Price	Material Loss	Inventory	Total
PROCESS A											
Material A											
Material B											
Material C											
Material D											
Subtotal:											
PROCESS B											
Material 1											
Material 2											
Subtotal:											
PROCESS C											
Material A	210,000	207,300	2,700	$38,000	$37,500	$37,500	$ 500	—	—	—	$ 500
Material B	366,700	400,000	(33,300)	22,000	25,000	24,000	(3,000)	1,000	—	—	(2,000)
Material C	26,400	40,000	(13,400)	1,320	2,000	2,000	(180)	—	—	(500)	(680)
Material D	40,800	40,000	800	6,120	6,000	6,000	120	—	—	—	120
Subtotal:	xxxxxx	xxxxxx	xxxxx	$67,440	$70,500	$69,500	$(2,560)	1,000	—	($500)	($2,060)
Plant Total	xxxx	xxxx	xxxx	$	$	$	$	$		$	$

In this report, the units are listed as well as values. The analysis of variance (gain or loss) shows the yield loss for in-process variations. These must always be balanced with the in-process control reports submitted by the manufacturing area.

The price column will show any variation from standard prices. The Material Loss would come from material loss reports.

An important area is the inventory gain or loss. This can measure the accuracy of the production reporting, transactions in the operations, thefts, or losses in interplant transfers, and any other area not covered by control reports.

These in-process reports, variance analysis, and related losses are a real opportunity to improve short-term financial results and return on capital employed. In the case where a manufacturer may be completing only 90 first quality units from each 100 units put into process, the plant is running extra time, personnel are being expended unnecessarily, and asset recovery is being reduced. In multi-plant operations it may be even possible to eliminate the necessity to construct an additional plant to supply the demand of sales growth simply by reduction of in-process, off-quality, and related losses.

For some industries, these off-quality or loss items which are saleable are placed on the market. Customers may even move them on to the end user resulting in complaints or deterioration of brand identification. Always, when off-quality merchandise is placed on the market for any reason, the lower price requested for these units tends to depress the prices obtainable on first quality merchandise.

The costs in financial accounting for this type of material should reflect the true loss. Normally, the loss is considered to be the total cost through the particular process minus the sales price. In most all cases, this is absolutely incorrect. The true loss is:

$$\text{True Off-Quality Loss} = \text{Selling Price First Quality} - \text{Selling Price Off-Quality.}$$

By using the difference between costs and selling prices of the merchandise, management fails to recognize the real loss in profit and other expenses associated with putting a first quality item on the market.

MAJOR PROCESS CONTROL

In addition to weekly and monthly reports, each major process requires a control by batch, roll number, manufacturing lot, major assembly, or other unit.

A Major Process Control Report is viewed in Figure 5–9. This gives prompt control over high cost operations without waiting for weekly or monthly analysis.

The machine hours, materials, and personnel can be measured quickly. In some cases, purchases, variable costs, and fixed costs will relate only to standard cost per machine hour.

FIGURE 5-9

Major Process Control Reports

Description		Machine Hours	Material A	Material B	Personnel	Purchases	Variable	Fixed	Total
Batch No. Part No.	Standard								
Pieces In	Actual								
Pieces Out	Variance								

Description		Machine Hours	Material A	Material B	Personnel	Purchases	Variable	Fixed	Total
Batch no. Part no.	Standard								
Pieces in	Actual								
Pieces out	Variance								

Every expense account requires a specification sheet. A typical one is contained in Figure 5–10.

Professional services fees should not be developed from last year's utilization or some expectation. They should be defined and specified on a systematic basis by project within the particular area of responsibility. The detailed worksheet should verify each expected need for outside services. It should include a description of the assignment, expected time period of the project for payment, justification, and approval.

FIGURE 5–10

Expense Specification Sheet

Account Name:	Professional Services	Year Ending:	xx/xx/xx
Account Number:	901	Person Responsible:	As Listed
Description of Account:		All fees paid for professional services— legal, auditors, management consultants, professional engineers, and similar outside services.	

Expense Item	Base Year	Last Year	This Year	Next Year
Professional Services:				
Manufacturing				
Distribution				
Sales and Merchandising				
Product Development				
Administration				
Total	___	___	___	___

Issued by:	Approved by:	Responsible Executive	Budget Year	Account No.

Billings for professional services should be in detail as listed in Figure 5–11 and Figure 5–12. On occasions, professional services—and particularly management consultants—like to deal with top executives and issue a billing for a lump sum amount. This practice should never be tolerated either by managers or financial accountants. Even when the manager or executive may approve an invoice for a lump sum amount, the Controller or financial area should request (through the manager responsible) a detailed billing.

Attorneys, auditors, engineers, and all outside services should be required to submit detailed billings specifying people, dates, and expenses.

Managers require a methodical approach to the approval of all expenses for any account. These should be specified and defined. Actual performance

FIGURE 5–11

Professional Services Billing

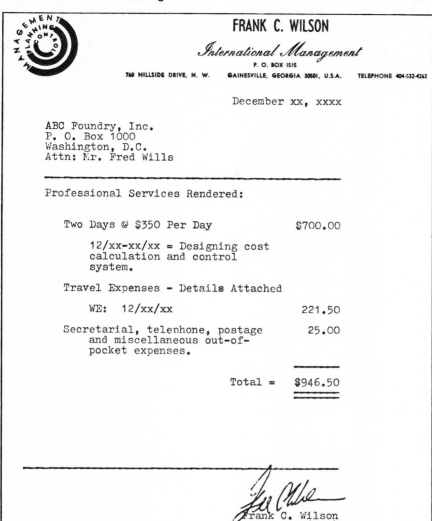

FRANK C. WILSON

International Management

P. O. BOX 1515

760 HILLSIDE DRIVE, N. W.   GAINESVILLE, GEORGIA 30501, U.S.A.   TELEPHONE 404-532-4262

December xx, xxxx

ABC Foundry, Inc.
P. O. Box 1000
Washington, D.C.
Attn: Mr. Fred Wills

Professional Services Rendered:

Two Days @ $350 Per Day	$700.00
12/xx-xx/xx = Designing cost calculation and control system.	
Travel Expenses - Details Attached	
WE: 12/xx/xx	221.50
Secretarial, telephone, postage and miscellaneous out-of-pocket expenses.	25.00
Total =	$946.50

Frank C. Wilson
P.E.   (CMC)

versus this plan should be compared. The same concentrated attention and follow-up should be given by management to the expenses of distribution, selling, merchandising, and administration as is given to manufacturing cost.

CORPORATE OR GROUP CHARGES

Larger firms with corporate or regional functions should make an extra effort to properly account for and insure effectiveness of corporate expenses.

First, the question should be asked, "Is this expense at the corporate level contributing to the effective and efficient operation of the business?" If not, then it should be eliminated.

FIGURE 5–12

Professional Services Expense Billing

ABC Foundry, Inc.

PRINT NAME & TITLE HERE--SIGN BELOW
Frank C. Wilson

LOCATION (TERRITORY-DISTRICT-REGION-DEPT.)
Gainesville, Ga. 30501

WEEK ENDING **12 /XX /XX**

EXPENSE ITEM	SUNDAY / /6	MONDAY / /6	TUESDAY / /6	WEDNESDAY / /6	THURSDAY / /6	FRIDAY / /6	SATURDAY / /6	TOTALS DOLLARS CENTS
1 BREAKFAST		− |−−	2 |00	2 |00				4	00
2 LUNCH		− |−−	− |−−	1 |00				1	00
3 DINNER		2 |00	3 |00	− |−−				5	00
4 HOTEL		13 |50	13 |50	− |−−				27	00
5								
6 TAXI & LIMO.								
7 TIPS								
8 TEL. & TEL.								
9								
10 TRANSPORTATION −Air		113 |00						113	00
11 −Car		11 |25		11 |25				22	50
12 ENTERTAINMENT								
13 Auto				49 |00				49	00
14 Rental								
15								
TOTALS ▶		139 |75	18 |50	63 |25				▶ 221	50

TRANSPORTATION DETAIL (SUPPORTING ITEM 10)

						ADVANCE
TRAVEL FROM	Gainesville, Ga.	Washington, D.C.				
TRAVEL TO	Washington, D.C.	Gainesville, Ga.				DUE COMPANY
ENDING SPEEDOMETER READING						
BEGINNING SPEEDOMETER READING						
TOTAL MILEAGE	75	75				DUE EMPLOYEE
TRANSPORTATION TICKET NUMBER						

APPROVAL	1. APPROVAL	2. APPROVAL	3. APPROVAL	4. ACCOUNT NUMBER

EXPLAIN BY ITEM NUMBER ANY UNUSUAL EXPENSE THAT MAY BE QUESTIONED. (OTHER THAN ENTERTAINMENT EXPENSES)

Item 4: Holiday Motel, Washington, D.C.
10: Air East Ticket #99 823 990 6
11: Mileage Gainesville, Ga. to Atlanta, Ga. Airport @ $0.15 per mile.
13: Eastern Auto Rental Ticket #21 923 774

PURPOSE OF TRIP: 2.00 Days = Traveling and working with Mr. Fred Wills and staff designing sales forecasting, stock status and production planning system for Plant #1.

X _Frank C. Wilson_
SIGNATURE

Corporate allocations can adversely affect cost control at the division or factory level. When the corporate office sends down an allocation for, say, $300,000, it is difficult for management at the factory level to understand why an arbitrary, lump sum $300,000 allocation is made to their plant. As a result, it may retard their enthusiasm to take action to make cost reductions of a few unnecessary people in the factory, a secretary in the office, or a clerk in distribution.

Corporate allocations should always be on a factual basis by cause. Sometimes, corporate allocations are distributed on percentage of sales, percentage of investment, or some other easy way. When they are distributed on a percentage of sales basis, this tends to encourage managers at the division level to lower their sales budgets simply to obtain a lower corporate expense allocation. When they are on a percentage of investment, a clever manager whose bonus is based on return on investment will delay an investment unnecessarily.

Corporate expenses should be charged to the division on a usage basis. This should be by exact expense account. This will encourage discipline at the corporate level to prevent the building of excessive staffs; it will increase validity at the division level, and more important, it will permit the division to place the corporate charges properly in their cost system.

RECOMMENDATIONS TO IMPROVE SHORT-TERM FINANCIAL MANAGEMENT

Managers should:

Set up a top management report with an overview of the financial operations and key variances to permit managers to ask the right questions and not be bogged down with too much detail.

Set up or improve departmental level cost control reports to permit responsible persons to have accurate and timely access to a full view of the controllable cost within their area of responsibility.

Institute or expand cost control reports over data processing and other similar service areas in the same manner as if they were production departments.

Concentrate cost control and management's attention on those few areas which have a significant impact on results; in one case it may be materials, in another case it may be purchases, in another it may be personnel, and another administrative expenses.

Monitor and reduce the in-process loss of materials from receiving to increase the packed first quality production.

Change the accounting for loss of off-quality production to show the real loss—profit as well as cost.

Set up timely process control over each element of major expenses.

Demand that corporate charges be reduced to a minimum. Managers should insist that these type expenses be detailed by cause and charged to divisions on a usage basis; and they should eliminate arbitrary allocations.

SUMMARY

Management must focus on manufacturing, maintain a low cost and high volume operation; then, manufacturing production operations can become a competitive edge in the market in the short term.

Management control reports for top management, middle management, department, and shift levels are displayed in this chapter. The value added concept is employed in these control reports. Detailed reports include material control, in-process yield, and quality control.

With inflationary changes in the economic environment coupled with fluctuating monetary values, managers can easily be deluded by financial results which may reflect growth as a result of economic or monetary distortions. Business results, at least internally, should be indexed and compared to base years to insure that managers are receiving reports that reflect true operating conditions, not distorted by financial manipulation.

An analytical, objective, and engineered approach is required for all expenses in the factory and at nonmanufacturing levels. The professional Industrial Engineering Department is a valuable asset in determining what costs should be, given conditions.

Averages, historical bases, percentages, and other unreliable ways should be eliminated from the business.

For the business in trouble, quick methods estimating costs and expenses may be used. A comparison of costs with those that exist in a reasonably efficient competitor or industry standard may be helpful. These empirical standards can then be followed by more precise ones engineered by professional personnel on a systematic basis. Precise standards developed at significant expense are of no value unless the firm weathers the short-term troubles and remains a viable business in the medium term.

Major processes, assembly lines, and other similar high cost and capital intense facilities require monitoring. Special control reports should be prepared for these activities.

It is essential to control manufacturing costs. The same analytical, engineered, and precise approach is required for expenses of distribution, selling, merchandising, and administration.

Control reports for materials, supplies, fuel, and other controllable expenses are displayed in this chapter. Special attention is given to data processing and professional services costs.

Corporate expenses allocated to plants, divisions, or regions are an excellent opportunity to increase cost and depress cost reductions at the lower levels. These expenses should be detailed and assigned to the divisions by cause rather than allocated on some arbitrary basis or percentage of sales, investment, or other easy way.

"Profit Improvement: Reducing Cost of Operations—Now" is the subject of Chapter Eight.

chapter SIX

Pricing

*Just give me the manufacturing cost; the price is set
by the market.*

Controlling the Product Mix and Sales Volume

THE MARKET PRICE is important in determining a selling price for a product. However, this factor does not reduce the validity or need for accurate costs throughout the system. By knowing the real cost, managers can select from the market potential those products which generate the most profit.

The difference between an average company and a superior one may be small, but it is all profit. In the academic world, there is no difference between a grade of 92 or 98; it is an "A." In business, the difference between 92 and 98 can be $600, $6,000, $6 million or more—all profit!

Of all the tasks of managers, pricing, control of the product mix, and timing of price changes are prime tasks.

DETERMINING PROFIT REQUIREMENTS

In many cases, firms use a percentage of sales as a profit markup—10 percent, 15 percent, or other unit. Wherever a percentage is utilized, it should be based on the return on capital employed by trade channel and product type. Those channels of distribution which have high stock requirements, long terms, and other cash consuming requirements call for larger percentages.

Some trade channels (large volume, private label, or wholesale) are expected to order in large quantities, to maintain inventories, and to pay invoices promptly. Should these functions be carried out by these channels of distribution, a lower percentage profit markup would be required to obtain the same return on capital employed in the business.

Sometimes, these customers do not carry out the required functions. Orders are placed in smaller quantities, longer terms are requested, and the supplier is expected to maintain an inventory to service incoming orders. In this situation, there is no reason or cause for a lower profit percentage markup for these type customers. In fact, in some instances, a higher percentage profit markup may be required to maintain the return on investment desired.

The percentage markup may be estimated based on capital employed as illustrated in Figure 6–1. In this example, two trade channels are displayed (Retail and Large Volume) with two categories of products using two different manufacturing processes.

FIGURE 6–1

Calculation of Investment
(dollars in thousands)

	Retail Channel		Large Volume		
	Category I	Category II	Category I	Category II	Total
Raw materials					
Raw Material A.............	$ 300		$ 100		$ 400
Raw Material B............		$ 350		$ 250	600
Work-in-process					
Raw Material A............	150		100		250
Raw Material B............		300		200	500
Finished goods					
Raw Material A............	800		200		1,000
Raw Material B............		1,300		400	1,700
Cash......................	100	200	50	150	500
Accounts receivable					
Product A.................	900	2,800			3,700
Product B.................			400	1,300	1,700
Plant and equipment					
Production Unit I...........	1,370	4,000	880	2,700	8,950
Production Unit II.........		1,350		910	2,260
Total...................	$3,620	$10,300	$1,730	$ 5,910	$21,560
25% Return on investment.....	$ 905	$ 2,580	$ 435	$ 1,480	$ 5,400
Sales $—Net.................	$7,000	$21,000	$4,600	$14,000	$46,600
Profit markup................	12.9%	12.3%	9.5%	10.6%	11.6%

The investment in inventories, accounts receivable, plant and equipment along with other needs for cash is listed.

Both Category I and Category II products for the retail channel have higher cash requirements. This is a result of the need for more finished goods inventory (make-to-stock, rather than make-to-order) to maintain excellent customer service. This example assumes that accounts receivable are financed, rather than factored (Chapter Ten, "Money Management").

The example in Figure 6–1 separates the plant and equipment by category of products. Two production units are involved. Production Unit I is utilized by both categories of products, whereas Category II products use the plant and equipment of Production Unit II only.

When the investment requirements are properly segmented, the difference in profit requirements by product category and channel of distribution can be determined. With the example in Figure 6–1, Retail, Category I products require a 12.9 percent of sales profit markup. Large Volume, Category I products need 9.5 percent. It is easy to see that the average in the "Total Column" (11.6 percent) is not correct for any product category or method of distribution.

Using averages of any type is dangerous and obsolete in this age of professional management. Superior managers know the true and important differences in costs and pricing requirements.

In many situations, where assembly lines and production units remain relatively constant regardless of the price or product being manufactured, a unit profit markup is more desirable than a percentage. Using the data contained in Figure 6–1 in relating it to units by trade channel and product type, the profit per unit can be determined as shown in Figure 6–2.

As an example, when the trends in automobile purchases shifted from large cars to smaller cars, the manufacturers produced a similar number of units. Yet, as a result of this product mix shift, the profits appeared to deteriorate rather sharply. In these cases, where the assembly line is the controlling factor in production, a per unit profit markup is needed for investment in plant, property, and equipment, while a percentage markup is required for inventories and accounts receivable.

The markups are used to develop the "Target Price" as illustrated in Chapter Four, Figure 4–1. This target price is not the selling price! It is another guide from which management can evaluate potential market prices.

FIGURE 6–2

Profit per Unit

	Retail		*Large Volume*	
	Category I	*Category II*	*Category I*	*Category II*
Profit planned (000)......................	$ 905	$2,580	$ 435	$1,480
Units—000...............................	2,000	4,000	2,000	5,000
Profit per unit...........................	$0.452	$0.645	$0.218	$0.296

Managers cannot base prices on manufacturing costs alone. Prices must be adjusted on the basis of competitive factors in the market, the company's specific market strategy, and its resources. This can lead to trouble in trying to attain predetermined profits where a range of products and different channels of distribution are involved. It calls for experience as well as judgment based on timely and accurate information in the market.

INTERCOMPANY PROFIT MARKUPS

When a particular situation develops where a large company has certain parts manufactured at one plant or division and other parts at another site, final manufacturing and assembly could be at still another location.

The handling of profit markups at each point of manufacture or assembly should be based on facts which cause the need for cash at each point—Division A, Division B, or Division C. The costs should be calculated through to the target selling price showing the profit markup required as an absolute amount. The costs and profit need to be transferred to the next assembly point in absolute amounts for inventory pricing and profit calculations.

Some firms have transferred products from Division A, say, to Division C, for final manufacturing and assembly with the profit markup concealed in the calculation. This simply leads to compounding profit in the final calculation. It can lead to a firm's developing a noncompetitive situation as well as accounting difficulties in interdivision profit eliminations.

In many industries, it is no longer possible to add profit at each point of manufacture or assembly. A company which tries to add profit at each investment or transactional point can be put into an obsolete or uncompetitive posture. Competitive pressures resulting from changing technology require a unified corporate strategy based on the long-term market position. Therefore, this dictates a comprehensive plan and understanding of how profits are handled throughout the business to achieve the best overall results.

An even more difficult situation arises when a firm requires several parts for final assembly into one item. Parts one and two may be manufactured internally, whereas part three may be purchased from outside suppliers. If the firm in its final assembly price uses an overall 10 percent markup or any other percentage, its manager will be saying to himself that he requires a 10 percent profit markup on sales manufactured internally to provide the return on investment for plant, property, equipment, and other financial needs. Likewise, 10 percent is desired on the portion purchased from outside suppliers.

It is clear in this situation that the outside supplier has already taken the profit. The final assembler cannot then compound it on the same basis with parts manufactured internally. It is necessary to build the profit markup into two parts: a markup required for items produced internally and a lesser amount for those purchased outside.

A lower profit markup is required on materials purchased from outside suppliers. The supplier has provided the plant, property, and equipment to produce the part. The final assembler needs to recover the return on capital employed in inventories and accounts receivable.

Accounting for internal transfers within divisions or between separate units is a complex process which requires policy decisions at the management level.

TRANSACTIONAL COST AND PRICING

Distributors, wholesalers, retailers, and similar merchants who purchase all or practically all of their merchandise from suppliers for resale have a special need to investigate the distortions resulting from percentage or gross margin pricing of products.

The example shown in Figure 6–3 is for a lower priced product.

Using the gross margin or percentage markup approach over landed factory cost, an item with a price of $36.50 has a gross margin markup of 30 percent. This adds $10.95 for a total distributor price of $47.45.

As the product moves through the channels of distribution from wholesaler to retailer, another percentage markup (30 percent) may be needed to arrive at a suggested retail selling price. In this example, this suggested retail price would be $61.69. The actual selling price would probably be adjusted to the $59.95 price point.

In fact, the wholesaler or distributor has a transactional cost for ordering the merchandise, placing it in the warehouse, entering the order, and shipping and delivering to the retailer. Converting the total profit requirements to a transactional cost of $5.00, and a transactional profit of $5.00 with a gross

FIGURE 6-3

Transactional Cost and Pricing for a Lower Priced Product

	Transactional Cost and Pricing	Gross Margin Pricing
Factory price............................	$36.50	$36.50
+ Transactional cost......................	5.00	x.xx
+ Transactional profit....................	5.00	x.xx
+ Gross margin..........................	3.65	10.95
Distributor price.........................	$50.15	$47.45
Retailer markup..........................	15.05	14.24
Retail price..............................	$65.20	$61.69
Target suggested selling price...........................	$64.95	$59.95

margin consideration for selling and other factors of $3.65, the distributor price becomes $50.15. The retailer markup of $15.05 moves the total suggested retail price to $65.20. Then, adjusting for price point considerations, the eventual selling price to the customer will be $64.95.

It is clear that with transactional cost and pricing, a higher price would be required than is expected under the gross margin or percentage considerations.

A reverse situation applies to the higher priced product illustrated in Figure 6–4. Using the same approach and concepts, the transactional cost in pricing approach would result in a selling price of $109.95. The gross margin approach needs a selling price of $114.95.

In this situation, gross margin and percentage markups underprice lower priced items and overprice higher priced merchandise. It is this approach which has led to conventional retailers losing a share of market to discount or economy stores. It has led better quality manufacturers with brand identification to lose shares of market to large volume and lower cost producers.

There is really little theoretical or practical argument to favor gross margin or percentage markups in any situation. Transactions and complexity cause cost. Inventories and accounts receivables generate needs for cash. A retailer selling a washing machine may require the same selling time to sell a cheap

FIGURE 6-4

Transactional Cost and Pricing for a Higher Priced Product

	Transactional Cost and Pricing	Gross Margin Pricing
Factory price............................	$ 67.50	$ 67.50
+ Transactional cost......................	5.00	x.xx
+ Transactional profit....................	5.00	x.xx
+ Gross margin..........................	6.75	20.25
Distributor price.........................	$ 84.25	$ 87.75
Retailer markup..........................	25.28	26.33
Retail price..............................	$109.53	$114.08
Target suggested selling price...........................	$109.95	$114.95

one as a high priced one. The installation cost for either may be identical. The delivery cost to the home of the customer is identical. Neither the delivery driver nor the truck employed recognizes that the contents delivered has a different value; it is a transaction and causes cost.

A similar situation exists with the retailer selling electrical appliances. The same installation and adjustment cost is required for an economical refrigerator or television set as for one with a higher cost.

Transactional cost calculation and transactional profit markups combined with percentage markups give manufacturers, wholesalers, distributors, retailers, and the entire channel of distribution (from raw material to a satisfied customer) the best opportunity to generate the desired return on capital employed. This method will give the right relationship between cause of cost and target selling price.

Percentage markups result in distortions. They cause manufacturers, distributors, and retailers to constantly seek higher sales volume and boost the sales of lower priced products. The exact opposite might be the best option. This statement does not ignore the fact that high volume, low cost operations —whether factories, distributors, or retail outlets—have a substantial competitive influence.

Generally, there are three levels of competition.

Level I: These competitors generally have higher quality, better service, larger cost, brand identification, more extensive advertising, and higher priced merchandise.

Level II: Competitors with medium quality merchandise, lesser service, increased volume, and lower cost operations generally fall into this level.

Level III: Competitors with low cost, low priced, high volume, reduced service, mass market, and promotional competitors with discount activities may be in this type competition.

Whether it is a manufacturer, wholesaler, retailer, or mail order business, the first policy of management is to determine, "Who is the competition?" Then, the business must be structured to be cost competitive and focused on that segment of the competition. Against Level I competition, a retailer may have a department store. Full line department stores in the Level I category of competition may have full, complete service, delivery, and repair. In order to compete with Level II and Level III competition, management of Level I operations would require an entirely different set of business characteristics to compete with the low cost, high volume, and little service merchandiser.

Transactional costing is only one aspect of answering the question, "Who is the competition?" It is necessary to understand the total market structure, especially when exporting. In a different market, a basic understanding of the "tiers" of distribution to enable the manufacturer or distributor to obtain better prices is essential. In almost every market, opportunities exist for those products within an intrinsic market value higher than the traditional cost of production to be obtained. This is especially true where new production techniques have been introduced.

Best pricing decisions are a combination of known costs and the competitive nature of the market. Transactional cost determination enables management to adopt the best pricing policy. *Transactional costing and pricing is an area the superior manager cannot afford to ignore, either in the organizational strategy, in the approach to competition, or in operating the business.*

A simplified sales and profit forecast is listed in Figure 6–5. The various items, such as materials, could be in much greater detail.

This summary gives the information available for estimating sales, profits, and break-even analysis. It also includes the key indicators to guide management—gross margin, value added, contribution, cash flow, and net profit.

FIGURE 6–5

Sales and Profit Forecast

Description	Value ($000)	Decision Points
Target sales	$50,000	
Less terms and discounts	4,000	
Net sales	$46,000	
Less materials	25,000	
Gross margin	$21,000	I
Less purchases	5,000	
Value added	$16,000	II
Less variable cost	3,000	
Contribution margin	$13,000	III
Less fixed cost	4,000	
Less depreciation	3,000	IV
Net profit	3,000	V
Less taxes	3,000	
Balance	0	
Number of units	13,000	

These data can be graphically displayed as shown in Figure 6–6. Figure 6–5 contains the conventional listing, that is, starting with sales and subtracting the various costs to arrive at a profit. It does separate net profits and taxes to the balance of "zero."

In fact, the statement should be reversed to show profits at the top and sales at the bottom. Then, emphasis would be in the right place, profits being the objective rather than sales volume. A properly oriented sales and profit forecast would be as shown in Figure 6–7.

FIGURE 6-6

Break-Even Chart

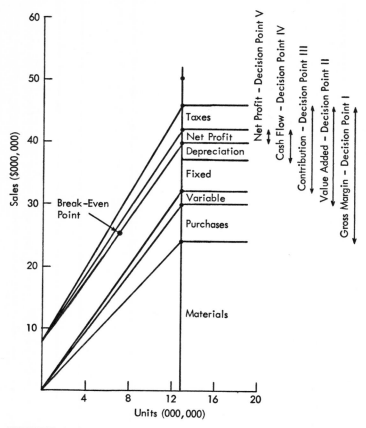

FIGURE 6-7

Sales and Profit Forecast
(reversed)

Description	Value ($000)	Decision Points
Number of units.........................	13,000	
Balance................................	$ 0	
Less taxes..............................	3,000	
Net profit..............................	3,000	V
Less depreciation.......................	3,000	IV
Less fixed cost.........................	4,000	
Contribution...........................	$13,000	III
Less variable cost......................	3,000	
Value added............................	$16,000	II
Less purchases.........................	5,000	
Gross margin...........................	$21,000	I
Less materials.........................	25,000	
Net sales..............................	$46,000	
Less terms and discounts................	4,000	
Target sales...........................	$50,000	

The graphic display for management (Figure 6–6) is plotted from the data in Figure 6–5. The key points are:

Description	Value ($000)	Decision Points
Gross margin	$21,000	I
Value added	16,000	II
Contribution margin	13,000	III
Cash flow	6,000	IV
Net profit	$ 3,000	V

A break-even point can be calculated and overlayed onto this chart. Of course, other types of charts can be drawn to place it on the chart without calculation.

From Figure 6–5, the contribution margin is $13 million for 13,000 units, or $1,000 per unit. With $7 million of fixed cost and $1,000 contribution per unit, 7,000 units will be required to cover the fixed costs.

With net sales of $46 million for 13,000 units, the price is nearly $3,540 per unit. For 7,000 units, then, the break-even point in sales dollars is $24,780,000. The break-even point can shift quickly as prices and conditions change.

VOLUME VARIATION

The problem with contribution analysis and break-even calculations is the assumption that fixed costs remain constant and variable costs change in a linear relationship. Often, the assumption is made that prices can be maintained at a higher volume.

In fact, fixed costs will increase as volume increases and prices or contribution margins may deteriorate as volume is added. Should a firm be on two-shift operations, three-shift operations may be achieved with limited added fixed cost—supervisory salaries, and so forth. However, if the firm is on three-shift operations, added capacity may well be needed for additional volume outside a limited range. For added volume where capacity exists, added capital expenditures may be needed to balance production for the higher volume.

There is no need to guess or for managers to make faulty assumptions on the fixed cost associated with volumes. These can be planned and estimated in advance.

Consider the example contained in Figure 6–8. The normal volume is 13,000 units. This example could be campers or some similar product.

At the normal volume, the profit per unit is $900. By lowering the volume to 10,000 units per year, and by more selective marketing, the contribution margin may be raised to $1,050 per unit. To attain an additional 1,000 units of sales, the contribution margin would be lowered to $800 per unit. As volume increases from 13,000 units to 19,000 units, the last 1,000 units would be sold at a contribution of $300 per unit.

The first 1,000 units can be attained with a small increase in fixed cost

FIGURE 6–8

Calculation of Added Volume Profit

	Contribution per Unit	Total Contribution ($000)	Fixed Cost ($000)	Profit ($000)	Total Profit ($000)
Volume					
10,000...............	$1,050	$10,500	$6,000	$4,500	$4,500
11,000...............	1,000	11,000	6,100	4,900	4,900
12,000...............	950	11,400	6,300	5,100	5,100
13,000...............	905	11,765	6,365	5,400	5,400
Added Volume					
+1,000...............	$ 800	$ 800	+$ 200	+$ 600	$6,000*
+1,000...............	700	700	+ 400	+ 300	6,300
+1,000...............	600	600	+ 800	− 200	6,100
+1,000...............	500	500	+ 1,000	− 500	5,600
+1,000...............	400	400	+ 200	+ 200	5,800
+1,000...............	300	300	+ 100	+ 200	6,000

* $5,400 + contribution for added volume.

($200,000). The third and fourth 1,000 additional units produced require added capacity, additional sales force, more administration, computer expansions, and other fixed costs.

In this example, the maximum profit can be achieved with the added volume of 2,000 units per year. Thereafter, the profit deteriorates. The firm is

FIGURE 6–9

Plot of Added Volume Total Profit

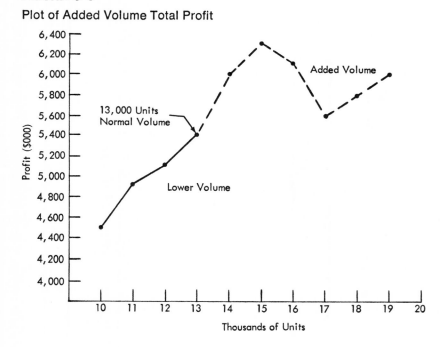

simply using up its plant and equipment to ship products without generating a profit.

Further, the striving for more sales volume is a downward pressure on prices in the market. The higher sales would require higher inventories and accounts receivable. At the higher sales volume (19,000 units), the return on capital employed would deteriorate rather drastically. Higher sales would require additional cash which would not generate added profits.

The profitability at the various levels of sales volume calculated in Figure 6–8 can be plotted in Figure 6–9. A graphical display of this type can point out the situation better than arithematical computations. This example is not theoretical. It is, with variations, factual in most every business situation. Managers must be extremely careful in using contribution analysis. It is a valuable tool for short-term analysis or volume variations, provided the assumptions relative to fixed cost, sales volume, and price are correct.

The real challenge to management is to move the profit curve upward (Figure 6–9). By controlling fixed cost, increasing productivity, and eliminating idle capacity, higher profits and return on investment can be achieved by developing new products that increase overall contribution.

PRODUCT TIERS

The various products in the mix should always be analyzed in "Product Tiers." These tiers could be based on profitability. Tier I would be products with superior profit opportunity; Product Tier II would be in the medium range; Tier III would be those products with possibly higher volume and lower financial results.

An example which relates to Figure 6–7, "Sales and Profit Forecast," is detailed in Figure 6–10. In this case, 3,000 units or 23 percent of the sales volume in units is generating the vast majority of the profit and contribution. These are Tier I products. Tier II products achieve significant volume and reasonable contribution. The Tier III products are contributors rather than profit earners. These could be promotional products, commodities, or other items required to maintain volume, entry into markets, or sales appeal.

In this example (Figure 6–10), the standard profit per year (Profit I) is $6 million. Profit II, using contribution analysis, is $8 million. This means that the products have shifted more to Tier I than planned in the normal volume. The full cost calculations for the product mix of 13,000 units remains correct for Profit I, $6 million.

Consider a slight change in the product mix as listed in Figure 6–11. Here, 1,000 units of Tier I products (Product 7) have shifted to 1,000 units of Tier III items (Product 3). A small shift in the product mix (as an example, from large cars to smaller cars, higher priced products to lower priced ones) can have a significant impact on financial results. Control of the product mix in a systematic, methodical, and analytical manner is essential. In this case, a small change of 7.6 percent of the units (without changing total unit

FIGURE 6-10

Sales and Profit Forecast Worksheet

	Units per Year	Actual Selling Price	Total Cost	Standard Profit per Unit	Standard Profit per Year ($000)	Variable Cost	Standard Contribution per Unit	Contribution per Year ($000)
Tier I								
Product 1.	1,000	$16,000	$14,500	$1,500	$1,500	$13,500	$2,500	$ 2,500
Product 7.	1,000	14,500	12,500	2,000	2,000	11,500	3,000	3,000
Product 9.	1,000	11,500	10,500	1,000	1,000	9,500	2,000	2,000
Tier II.								
Product 2.	2,000	10,500	$10,000	500	1,000	9,500	1,000	2,000
Product 5.	2,000	9,500	9,000	500	1,000	8,500	1,000	2,000
Product 8.	2,000	8,500	8,000	500	1,000	7,500	1,000	2,000
Tier III.								
Product 3.	1,000	7,000	$ 7,500	(500)	(500)	7,000	0	0
Product 4.	2,000	6,000	6,500	(500)	(1,000)	5,500	500	1,000
Product 6.	1,000	5,500	5,500	0	0	5,000	500	500
	13,000				Profit I = $6,000		Fixed cost =	$15,000
								7,000
							Profit II =	$ 8,000

FIGURE 6–11

Sales and Profit Forecast Worksheet
(with slight change in the product mix)

	Units per Year	Actual Selling Price	Total Cost	Standard Profit per Unit	Standard Profit per Year ($000)	Variable Cost	Standard Contribution per Unit	Contribution per Year ($000)
Tier I								
Product 1	1,000	$16,000	$14,500	$1,500	$1,500	$13,500	$2,500	$ 2,500
Product 7	0	14,500	12,500	2,000	0	11,500	3,000	0
Product 9	1,000	11,500	10,500	1,000	1,000	9,500	2,000	2,000
Tier II								
Product 2	2,000	10,500	10,000	500	1,000	9,500	1,000	2,000
Product 5	2,000	9,500	9,000	500	1,000	8,500	1,000	2,000
Product 8	2,000	8,500	8,000	500	1,000	7,500	1,000	2,000
Tier III								
Product 3	2,000	7,000	7,500	(500)	(1,000)	7,000	0	0
Product 4	2,000	6,000	6,500	(500)	(1,000)	5,500	500	1,000
Product 6	1,000	5,500	5,500	0	0	5,000	500	500
	13,000				Profit I = $3,500			$13,000
							Fixed cost =	7,000
							Profit II =	$ 6,000

volume at all) dropped the expected profits (Profit II) by 25 percent or $2 million.

These examples demonstrate the need for using contribution analysis for estimating the effect of short-term changes of price, volume, or product mix. In Figure 6–10, the standard profit (Profit I) remains $6 million as planned. Yet, in Figure 6–11, Profit I drops to $3,500,000 while the number of units remains 13,000. This is a result of a shift of higher contribution products to those with lower contribution. A shift of this magnitude would invalidate the total cost calculations and require a revision of cost data.

The utilization of product tiers for analysis can be an added supplement to product classifications (Chapter Three, Figure 3–1). *Product planning, product analysis, product mix control, and pricing are a real opportunity for superior managers to move ahead of competitors. A planned, systematic, and analytical approach is absolutely essential to achieving superior results in the immediate future.*

MANAGING IN A SHORTAGE ECONOMY

Wherever shortages exist, whether these be productive capacity, raw materials, or other items necessary for producing a product, contribution analysis is an excellent tool for improving short-term financial results.

Where materials or energy are in short supply, they should be allocated to those products, those customers, and those channels of distribution which will give the best financial return. This cannot be done completely. It is always necessary to maintain a sufficient balance with products, customers, and distribution methods to achieve growth and maintain financial results when the shortage condition has passed.

Shortage does not necessarily imply raw material inadequacies. Personnel may also be difficult to obtain. Anywhere personnel are in short supply, the product mix might be moved into areas with higher value added through technology or productive resources to fully utilize the people available.

In complex situations, linear programming is an excellent tool to give better utilization of materials and resources in shortage situations. Managers must insure that the assumptions included in the mathematical calculations are valid as time and conditions change.

Managing in a shortage economy requires an understanding of the total business resources. Use of linear programming techniques is sometimes related to manufacturing characteristics only. The availability of capital and the cost of money utilized must always be considered optimization calculations. Further, marketing assumptions must consider the long-range effects on the firm. It may be possible in a shortage situation to eliminate certain customers or channels of distribution. In most cases, shortages are temporary. This requires that management be very careful in making short-term decisions relative to customers, distribution methods, or products which will be required for growth in sales and profits when the shortage no longer exists.

Because of uncertainty, the most difficult problem for managers is developing a systematic method that accurately estimates sales and profits. It is not always possible in advance to specify the volume or determine the price which can be obtained. In this situation, alternatives must be evaluated.

First, the price ranges are classified:

1 = Lowest price
2 = Average price
3 = Highest price.

Then, the volume ranges can be defined:

A = Highest volume
B = Average volume
C = Lowest volume.

Consider the product and alternatives arrayed in Figure 6–12. Given a fixed cost of $2,900,000, the alternative financial results would be as listed in Figure 6–13.

FIGURE 6–12

Calculation of Variable Contribution with Uncertainty

Product	Sales Range	Sales in Units	Variable Contribution Range	Variable Contribution per Unit	Variable Contribution ($000)		
1	A	3,900	1	$600	A1—$2,340	B1—$2,160	C1—$1,800
	B	3,600	2	$700	A2— 2,730	B2— 2,520	C2— 2,100
	C	3,000	3	$800	A3— 3,120	B3— 2,880	C3— 2,400
2	A	1,400	1	$740	A1—$1,036	B1—$ 888	C1—$ 592
	B	1,200	2	$840	A2— 1,176	B2— 1,008	C2— 672
	C	800	3	$940	A3— 1,316	B3— 1,128	C3— 752
3	A	250	1	$700	A1—$ 175	B1—$ 140	C1—$ 70
	B	200	2	$750	A2— 188	B2— 150	C2— 75
	C	100	3	$850	A3— 213	B3— 170	C3— 85

The combination of highest volume and highest price (condition A3, Figure 6–13) would generate the highest profit of $1,749,000. From Figure 6–12, the sum of variable contribution for A3 conditions is $3,120,000 or $1,316,000, plus $213,000, or $4,649,000 (Figure 6–13). Subtracting the fixed cost of $2,900,000, the estimated profit would be $1,749,000.

The lowest volume and lowest price (C1) would generate the lowest profit or, in this case, a loss of $440,000. With data put together in this manner, management can use its intuition and judgment of the market to determine the best, lowest, and most likely profit expectations when managing in an uncertain environment. This approach is particularly helpful for a marginal firm or one in a crisis. It can guide managers in determining the severity of the crisis and magnitude of potential loses. With the known range

FIGURE 6-13

Profit Estimate with Volume and Price Changes

Volume/Price Condition	A1	A2	A3	B2	B2	B3	C1	C2	C3
Units................................	5,550	5,550	5,550	5,000	5,000	5,000	3,900	3,900	3,900
Variable contribution (000)..........	$3,551	$4,094	$4,649	$3,188	$3,678	$4,158	$2,462	$2,847	$3,237
Fixed cost (000).....................	2,900	2,900	2,900	2,900	2,900	2,900	2,900	2,900	2,900
Profit estimate ($000)..............	$ 651	$1,194	$1,749	$ 288	$ 778	$1,258	($ 438)	($ 53)	$ 337

of financial results, the risk involved can be approximated to guide short-run expendable decisions to improve operations.

Managers should:

RECOMMENDA-TIONS TO IMPROVE SHORT-TERM FINANCIAL MANAGEMENT

Review existing methods of determining desired profit markups. Where practical, profit calculations using percentages should be eliminated. Profits should be determined based on cause of cost or capital employed. Cause-of-cost transactional analysis is essential to develop an amount per unit in conjunction with percentage on capital employed to arrive at the suggested selling price.

Set up sales and profit forecasts so that adequate differentiation can be made for multiple control points—gross margin, value added, contribution, cash flow, and net profit.

Draw up logically and analyze the effect of change in sales volume on expected profits. Give adequate compensation for changes which may occur in fixed cost.

Place all products in profit tiers based on profitability and contribution. Analyze the product mix based on potential changes in the short term.

Monitor and control the product mix to avoid a shift from higher contribution items to those with lower contribution margins.

Concentrate on moving a small number of units from low contribution items to those with higher contributions which will have a significant impact on profits.

Analyze the capital invested by product. Low contribution items can have a satisfactory financial return if low inventories are required and customer terms of payment are short which enable a quick recovery of the cash.

Plan and manage the business which is operating under conditions of uncertainty and shortages by using the best analytical and objective information available based on sound assumptions to maintain the viability of the business in the short-term.

SUMMARY

The determination of profit markups required to generate the desired return on capital employed is a prime task of managers. Percentages should be avoided wherever practical.

Transactions cause cost and require profit. Examples illustrate how profit can be applied on a transactional basis to more correctly price products.

In many cases, profit per unit is needed. By using units or transactional bases, managers can overcome the possibility of underpricing low priced products and overpricing higher quality items. The danger of mispricing can occur with a wide variety of products and trade channels by utilizing percentages, gross margin, or contribution markups.

Sales and profit forecasts are contained in these pages along with chart analyses of the key points for management control—gross margin, value added, contribution, cash flow, and net profit.

Direct costing theory or contribution analysis assumes that variable costs change in linear relationship while fixed costs remain constant. This is usually not true. An example of how to evaluate expected profit with changes in volume is illustrated in this chapter. It demonstrates the fallacy of constantly striving for added sales volume unless the assumptions on fixed costs and prices are valid relative to competition.

Managing in the shortage economy is discussed. The advantages of linear programming and related pitfalls when faulty assumptions are utilized are explained.

A method of dividing products into tiers based on profit expectations and using these tiers as a basis for management planning of the product mix in the short term is included for consideration. Control and realignment of the product mix is an important opportunity to quickly improve financial results. Because of uncertainty, the most difficult problem for managers is developing a systematic method that accurately estimates sales and profits. A method of using product groups combined with various ranges of sales volume and contribution range is shown. This permits management to use their own intuition and judgment to determine the lowest, highest, or most likely profitability under uncertain conditions.

section three

Inventory Management
Profit Improvement

chapter SEVEN

Inventory Management

We have two million units of inventory. Yet, we are not delivering the merchandise. WHY?

Practical Techniques to Obtain Higher Sales and Lower Inventories

ONE OF THE BEST OPPORTUNITIES to improve short-term financial management in almost every business is inventory control.

Inventories, from raw materials at the factory to finished goods in outlying distribution warehouses, can be a chief consumer of cash. Although wide variations exist, $0.20 to $0.40, or even more, can be required per dollar of sales to finance inventories.

These inventories can tie up much of the firm's assets. They can cause high interest expense for firms which are underfinanced or for those which must borrow funds to finance sales growth in business operations. In some businesses, it has been necessary to slow sales as a result of the inability to finance additional inventories—inventories required to service customers at a higher sales volume level.

Inventories can cause radical change in financial results, both up and down. In times of inflation and increasing prices, false inventory gains can occur. These become real financial improvements only when the goods are sold. Financial results for tax purposes require constant attention to inventory pricing and methods of inventory accounting. In inflationary times, Lifo (last in, first out) increases the cost of sales. Earnings are thereby depressed and tax payments reduced. The Fifo (first in, first out) inventory accounting plan accomplishes a similar purpose in the downward cycle.

The more dangerous effect of inventories on financial results is the potential for inventory losses. In times of declining prices, inventory write-downs can occur. Even in normal times, the necessity to write-down obsolete or discontinued merchandise can be a serious drain on achieving superior financial performance.

At the starting point, good inventory management is not systems. It is organization. It is assigning responsibility for inventories (Chapter Two, Figure 2–4, Distribution Services).

The next step is product management (Chapter Three). These matters fall within the area of management policy.

If management insists on having a complex product line with multiple outlying warehouses, inventories can be expected to be high. Therefore, the

117

return on investment in the firm will be lowered. By focusing on the fewest products which concentrate on the strengths of the manufacturing resources available and efficient distribution, the foundation for sales forecasting, production, and inventory control systems can be simplified. Development of a system is, for practical purposes, a mechanical function. Systems and procedures should never be expected to replace management policies.

Management must decide what level of customer service is needed to serve customer needs relative to competition. It is a management decision which will standardize products to reduce complexity in transactions. Systems and procedures in themselves will not reduce inventory. They will provide the information and control points from which management can make decisions and take actions on those factors which cause inventory. These are product complexity, customer service levels, lead times in manufacturing, number of outlying warehouse points, sales volume per stockkeeping item, and related factors.

FORECASTING

The first step in improving inventory management systems is in forecasting. Basically, managers have five needs for forecasts, predictions, or estimates of future demand:

1. Medium- and long-range market forecasts for business planning of capacity and capital expenditures.
2. Short-range stockkeeping item forecasts for production planning, customer service, and inventory control.
3. Basic market research to seek out causes of present and future demand.
4. Methods of predicting short-run "turns" in economic conditions and markets.
5. Determination of sales by trading area for sales quotas.

There are different forecasting techniques which will serve each of these needs best. Unit forecasts are needed. Dollar or value forecasts vary too greatly as a result of inflation, price changes, currency revisions, and other factors not associated with the primary product basis—units.

Long-Range Forecasts

Even while concentrating on near-term expectations, the manager must look ahead to find out what the future holds for the products and markets of the firm. Medium- and long-range forecasts give a perspective unattainable from short-range outlooks. The market may be declining, as an example, to a point where the firm should be sold or liquidated. It could be that growth in the years ahead dictates abnormal risks now to be ready for future opportunities. Longer-range forecasts can indicate when to gear up for an upturn or cut back for a cyclical slowdown in the short term.

For long-range market forecasts (two or more years in advance), time series analysis can be a help. Mathematical formulas available in many texts for time series analysis generally include the components illustrated in Figure 7–1.[1]

This example indicates a linear trend of basic demand which may be up or down. The trend component is not necessarily linear. It may follow some other mathematical function, particularly in periods of rapid growth or decline.

The seasonal segment is the change from normal within a one-year time period. As an example, normal sales may be 1,000 units per month. In one month, October as an example, the expected sales could be 1,200 units. The seasonal ratio would be 1,200 divided by 1,000, or 1.20.

FIGURE 7–1

Long-Range Forecast Use Trend Analysis

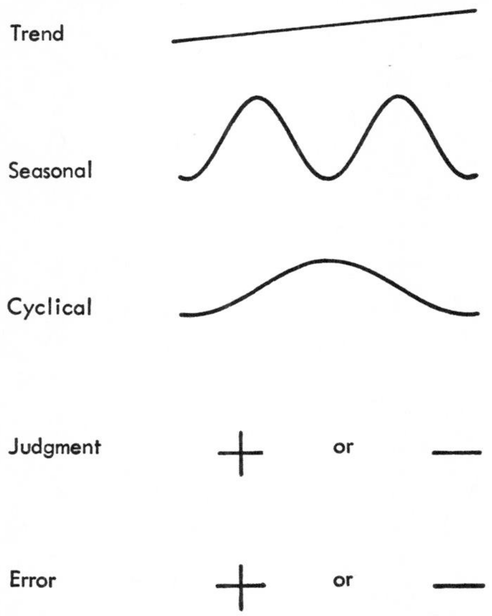

Trend

Seasonal

Cyclical

Judgment   + or —

Error   + or —

The cyclical component generally adjusts for business cycles over a three- to five-year time interval. During the 60s with explosive growth in many industries, the study of cycles was secondary.

In addition to the cyclical element, studies indicate the influence of longer waves in the economies of western capitalism over a period of decades.[2] Most forecasting techniques have not considered these longer waves in the economy.

A table of a medium-range forecast using time series analysis is displayed in Figure 7–2.

---

[1] Edward C. Bryant, *Statistical Analysis*, 2d ed. (New York: McGraw-Hill Book Company, 1966), pp. 182–211.

[2] James B. Shuman, *The Kondratieff Wave* (New York: World Publishing, 1972), pp. 25–41.

FIGURE 7–2

Medium-Range Forecast Based on Time Series Analysis
(in millions of units)

Year	Quarter	Product I	Product II	Product III	Product IV	Product V	Industry Total
Actual shipments—prior year							
19xx	Total	734	34	44	44	78	934
Estimated shipments—current year							
19xx	Actual 1	195	8	13	14	21	251
	Actual 2	205	9	16	13	20	263
	Actual 3	205	8	12	12	19	256
	Estimate 4	210	8	12	10	20	260
	Total	815	33	53	49	80	1,030
Predicted shipments							
19xx	Total	820	30	55	40	85	1,030
19xx	Total	890	25	60	45	90	1,110
19xx	Total	1,000	25	60	50	90	1,225

In this example, large growth has occurred from the prior year to the current year. A cyclical slowdown is expected in the next year ahead with growth resuming for the second and third years in the future. Forecasts of this type can be prepared on an annual, quarterly, monthly, or other time period basis.

It is important to adjust all forecasts for judgment or empirical knowledge of the market. Although it is not shown in this figure, long-range forecasts can be extrapolated with probability limits for expected deviations.

Most time series analysis mathematical formulas are based on the assumption that history will repeat itself. This implies that the conditions which existed during the time period of the data utilized will repeat into future years. In the international economy and many domestic markets, rapid changes in monetary, political, and social factors take place which invalidate the basic assumption of time series analysis. This is where management judgment must be applied. Managers must detect changes in trends which will affect future years' markets.

Price elasticity (Chapter Three) is a factor which could change the trend in many markets. This involves a change in demand for a particular product. It could include shifts from one product to a substitute product due to price, operating cost, or other factor.

When selling prices are increased from prior years, the slope of the trend line may be lowered. When real earnings of consumers decline, funds must be expended on essential needs—food, clothing, and such expenses. In this case, the purchase of postponable, consumer merchandise (carpets, automobiles, appliances, and other big ticket items) will be delayed, for customers may trade down to lower priced products.

In studying long-term expectations, we should not be detracted from the short term. Economists and others who forecast long-range results are plentiful. The need is for managers and market analysts to guide decisions in the next three to six months or at most 12 to 18 months. This, of necessity, involves more risks—risks that many fear to accept.

The real needs for short-term inventory management are forecasting systems and techniques which help predict demand by stockkeeping item—product, size, color, package, or other unique characteristic.

Many firms request each salesman to prepare his forecasts by trading area. Independent of this approach is the need for a specific method of forecasting for production planning and inventory control.

Where sufficient random demand exists, exponential smoothing is the best mathematical method. As shown in Figure 7–3, exponential smoothing

FIGURE 7–3

Short-Range Forecast by Stockkeeping Item Conventional Average and Exponential Average

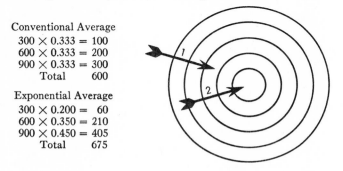

Conventional Average
300 × 0.333 = 100
600 × 0.333 = 200
900 × 0.333 = 300
Total   600

Exponential Average
300 × 0.200 = 60
600 × 0.350 = 210
900 × 0.450 = 405
Total   675

is much like zeroing in a rifle. A forecast is made, an error occurs when compared to actual results; then, an adjustment is made. The arithmetic to achieve these forecasts varies from very simple to extremely complex formulations. For practical purposes, these methods give more weight to current statistics and thereby improve the timeliness of forecast over conventional averages. Many publications and much literature exist for those wishing more in-depth study of exponential smoothing. It is, in simple language, a different kind of weighted average.

The key to any system is the ability of the people operating the system to understand the logic and results. It is always better to have a simple system well understood with a bit of inaccuracy, rather than a very sophisticated, mathematically precise one which may not significantly improve forecast performance or be understood.

A simplified forecast for a manual system may be as indicated in Figure 7–4. This one is based on 13 four-week periods per year, rather than months. Using 13 periods rather than 12 months, the same number of selling days exist in each period. Further, there is no need to adjust for those systems

FIGURE 7-4

Detailed Forecast by Item

Period:	1	2	3	4	5	6	7	8	9	10
Seasonal Factor:	0.90	1.05	1.10	0.95	0.90	0.85	0.90	1.05	1.15	1.25
Date:	2/2/xx	3/2/xx	3/30/xx	4/27/xx	5/25/xx	6/22/xx	7/20/xx	8/17/xx	9/14/xx	10/12/xx
Product *Category*										
Westwood										
Actual..................	750	900	787	800	650	563	...	...	...	...
Forecast..............	...	...	787	765	684	631	668	779	853	928
Error...................	...	...	...	+	–	–	...	...	...	...
Actual—deseasonalized.............	833	857	715	842	722	662	...	...	...	...
Average...............	...	...	...	805	760	742	...	...	...	...
Mediterranean Tile										
Actual..................	2,500	3,500	4,000	2,000	3,500	1,500	...	...	...	...
Forecast..............	...	...	...	3,087	2,722	2,048	2,327	2,715	2,994	3,232
Error...................	...	...	...	–	+	–	...	...	...	...
Actual—deseasonalized.............	...	...	...	2,105	3,889	1,765	...	...	...	...
Average...............	...	...	...	3,249	3,025	3,210	2,586	...	...	...

FIGURE 7–5

Forecast Worksheet

Date: xx/xx/xx   Warehouse: Dallas   Page 82

Color: 20   Name: Brass   Width: 12 ft–0 in.   Model No.: 1740   Name: Colonial

	May	June	July	August	September	October	November	December	January	February	March	April
Number of weeks........	4	4	5	4	4	5	4	4	5	4	4	5
Seasonal factors........	1.05	1.00	.90	1.00	1.10	1.20	1.00	.85	.85	.90	1.00	1.15
Export estimates.......												
Judgment factors.......	1.00	1.00	1.00	1.00	1.00	1.00	1.00	1.00	1.00	1.10	1.20	1.30
Promotional estimates...											1,500	2,000
Contract estimates......												
Actual orders.........	744	208	313	1,131	303	596						
Forecast.............	756	716	634	412	589	678	432	367	459	427	2,018	2,807
Error...............	12–	508–	321–	412	286–	82–						
Weekly average........	179	141	103	134	113	108						
Control factor........						1.00–						

Color: 30   Name: Copper   Width: 48 in.   Model No.: 1740   Name: Colonial

	May	June	July	August	September	October	November	December	January	February	March	April
Number of weeks........	4	4	5	4	4	5	4	4	5	4	4	5
Seasonal factors........	1.05	1.00	.90	1.00	1.10	1.20	1.00	.85	.85	.90	1.00	1.15
Export estimate........	.00	.00	.00	.00	.00	.00	.00	.00	.00	.00	.00	.00
Judgment factors.......												
Promotional estimates...												
Contract estimates......												
Actual orders.........	408	301	250	674	235	807						
Forecast.............	415	392	409	268	382	456	388	329	412	349	388	557
Error...............	7–	91–	159–	268	147–	351						
Weekly average........	98	91	67	87	76	97						
Control factor........						1.35						

which use four- or five-week months. This example is a conventional moving average adjusted for seasonal effects only.

Errors are detected by visual observation or runs of "plus" or "minus" beyond statistical probability expectations.

An exponential smoothing system for larger firms with complex product lines and computer availability is contained in Figure 7–5. This forecast system compensates for four- and five-week months as well as seasonal averages. It can be adjusted for selling days or other meaningful bases.

The estimate itself is a sum of the exponentially smooth forecast, including seasonal component adjusted for sales, and marketing judgment to override the mathematical forecast (judgment factor). Provision is included for export estimates, expected market promotions, contract, or made-to-order requirements.

The control factor is a statistical calculation to determine when the forecast is within mathematical control. This permits only the exceptions to be printed out for adjustment by the Market Research Department.

This particular display (Figure 7–5) is for a regional warehouse. It could be for a salesman's territory or sales manager's region. They can be combined to form a consolidated forecast—either for central plant manufacturing, or scheduling outlying assembly operations. Data printouts of this type can give sales and marketing managers more information from which to develop their own sales forecasts.

For larger customers, the supplying firm could produce a sales forecast by customer. Very frequently, these internally produced forecasts are more accurate guides to customer demand than estimates provided from the customer. Larger customers sometimes overforecast demand with the thought that the supplier will produce the merchandise. Then, it will be held in the supply warehouse at the supplier's expense and immediately available to the end using customer for filling orders.

An important advantage of exponential smoothing is the relatively limited past history required to implement or begin operations of a system. Further, less data storage is required for computerized systems employing exponential smoothing. In addition to the averaging, trend, seasonal, and other factors can be included in the equation.

The foundation for production planning and inventory control is accurate forecasting within the time period of the production plan. More precise forecasts permit the right quantity of products to be manufactured. Accurate forecasts reduce the safety stocks required throughout the system from manufacturing through distribution to final delivery to the customer.

Other Forecast Techniques

For basic market research, multiple regression analysis is a mathematical tool for consideration. Normally, this relates leading indicators statistically to produce a forecast of future demand. Leading indicators may be:

X_1 = New housing starts.
X_2 = Discretionary income per household.
X_3 = Mobile home assemblies.
X_4 = Automobile sales.
X_5 = Competing product sales.

The leading indicators are many and varied by industry. They should always have a relationship to the product being forecast. Sometimes statisticians may find a leading indicator which mathematically correlates with past sales. Yet, it may have no known relationship. Variables included in multiple regression or correlation analysis must always be verified by management as reliable indicators for future demand.

Replacement requirements in some products can be a major part of future demand statistics. This requires the calculation of the replacement cycle and elasticity of shifts in the cycle. Autocorrelation, the relationship of shipments to prior years, is a mathematical approach to aid the estimating of future replacement requirements. As an example, consider a consumer product where the wearout replacement due to relocation of families or change as a result of styling may occur in four, five, or six years. Autocorrelation techniques can be employed to compare demand for the earlier time periods with subsequent statistics to arrive at the best replacement cycle.

Econometric models and complex techniques can involve large outlays of money which will not contribute to short-term improvements in performance. These should be delayed in a crisis until the long-range future is assured.

A diffusion index is a good method of isolating "turns" in business or economic conditions which may affect the business in the immediate future. These also use leading indicators, such as:

1. Consumer confidence statistics.
2. Inflation ratio.
3. Interest rates.
4. Consumer savings.
5. Average manufacturing work week.
6. Inventories at manufacturers and in distribution channels.

These can be plotted with control limits as indicated in Figure 7–6. The diffusion index ratios can be included in short-term forecasting techniques as another component to improve forecast accuracy. The important fact is to detect changes in trends which will influence decisions in the coming months.

For individual firms, statistics exist to develop an internal diffusion index. These statistics may be:

1. Orders received.
2. Bad debts.
3. Accounts receivable.
4. Merchandise assigned but not shipped.
5. Inventory available.

FIGURE 7–6

Diffusion Index Chart

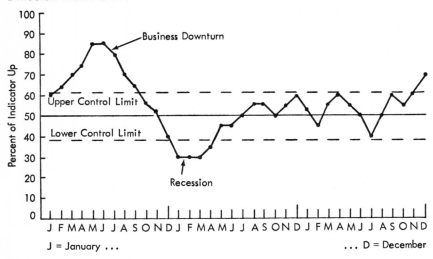

The problem with multiple regression analysis, diffusion indexes, and other techniques utilizing leading indicators is finding a statistic which reflects lead demand for the product in question. It is necessary to insure that the lead time (one month, two months, and so on) remains reasonably constant. Statistics on consumer confidence have been included in many forecasts as a leading indicator. In some time intervals, consumer confidence ratios would change gradually and move up significantly over a three- to nine-month time period. At other times (as an example, with the oil embargo, political turmoil, or monetary instability), consumer confidence statistics would vary substantially over very short periods of time. Surveillance of any data element utilized as a leading indicator must be constantly maintained to verify its validity. Forecasting is not, as commonly believed, largely a study of data and statistics. It is necessary to consider the psychology of economics[3] and how consumers responses change with news events, political turmoil, or other factors.

Other forecast techniques include simulation, input-output models, survey techniques, ratio analysis, sampling methods, econometric models, or other ways of improving management judgment.

Forecasting New Products

Probably the most troublesome aspect of production planning and inventory control is new products, or in the case of automobiles, the number of units which may be sold with a particular option, such as stereo tape players, for which past history is lacking.

Using past statistics of new products by category or known relationship,

[3] Katoma, George, *Psychological Economics*, (New York: Elsevier Scientific Publishing Co., Inc., 1975), pp. 76–32.

FIGURE 7-7

Curves for Forecasting New Items

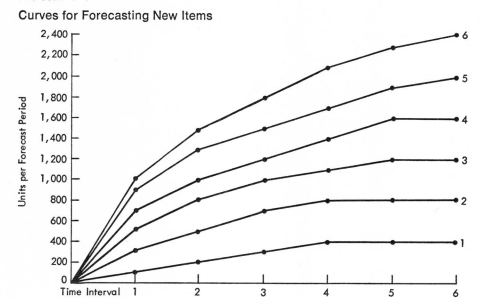

curves can be developed as shown in Figure 7–7. This chart lists categories one through six. These may vary by price point, model characteristic, or other factor. Then, when a new product or item is placed into the line, management or marketing can determine into which category the new item may fall. The curve can be selected to be built in either manually or automatically to the forecast system. At each forecast interval until the system becomes accurate, the forecast can be manually reviewed, the curve shifted, or judgment adjustment applied to improve forecast accuracy.

New product introduction demand curves are essential to improving production planning and inventory control of new items. The development of new product curves or other methods of estimating sales for new items brings an analytical element of discipline through the introduction of products which can reduce the potential for failure. These also provide a basis for comparison of actual results to the estimate upon introduction of the new product.

INVENTORY PLANNING

Given the forecast input, a stock status by warehouse or consolidated operation can be listed as indicated in Figure 7–8. This report shows the total finished inventory, items assigned to orders, merchandise in transit, back orders, future orders within the lead time or reordering, and memo future orders outside the reorder lead time.

The reorder point is determined based on the weeks of lead time, service level, and forecast error. The reorder point tells when to reorder. The lead time demand can be determined from the economic order quantity, the

FIGURE 7-8

Stock Status

Date xx/xx/xx   Warehouse: Dallas

Color	Total Finished Inventory	Assign to Orders	In Transit	Back Orders	Future Orders	Memo Future Orders	Net Available Inventory	Reorder Point	Lead Time Demand	To Order — Square Yards	To Order — Linear Yards	To Order — Rolls	Minimum Inventory	Over-(Under-) stock	Average Wkly. Estimated Sales	Weeks of Inventory
Model No.: 1740															**Name: Colonial**	
10	325						325	111	165				120	160	32	10
20	120		245				120	392	576	456	342	4	284	(164)	108	1
30	881		140				881	322	486				225	395	97	9
40	844						844	149	188				126	656	23	37
50	0			241			241—	348	504	745	558	6	256	(497)	92	2
60	685						685	1,096	1,614	929	696	8	791	(106)	305	6
70	572	120					452	1,042	1,212	760	570	6	942	(490)	100	5
Total	3,427	120		241			3,066						2,744	1,211 / (1,257)	757	
Model No.: 1800															**Name: House and Garden II**	
10	1,461						1,461	159	235				140	1,227	45	32
15	0	140	245	105			140	200	295				144	(4)	56	4
20	665	259	140				665	145	238	155	116	1	140	432	55	15
25	1,464						1,205	440	567				365	638	75	20
30	457						457	163	251				140	206	52	9
35	751	140					611	204	295				150	316	54	14
40	913						913	236	280				210	633	26	35
45	955			140			815	268	346				222	469	46	21
50	108						108	85	137				140	(55)	31	3
60	237						237	63	105				140	132	25	9
70	712						712	220	366				140	346	86	8
Total	7,727	539	385	245			7,324						1,931	4,399 / (59)	551	15

practical amount required to prevent excessive reorders or amounts to prevent excessive recycling of production. A minimum inventory is listed and overstocked conditions are pinpointed. Average weekly sales and weeks of inventory are included.

Business operations without computers (wholesalers, warehouses, and others) may use a simplified report as illustrated in Figure 7–9. In cases where statistical forecasting systems are available, reorder points, lead time demand, and inventory levels should be calculated. The use of "inventory turns" is a helpful guide. Inventory turn statistics are easy to arrive at arithmetically. However, they can be misleading.

The inventory required to maintain customer service is directly related to sales volume per stockkeeping item, to service level desired for customers by marketing, to errors in the forecast, and to definable parameters.

A key element of information is "overstocked." Stock status reports of the type indicated in Figure 7–8 or Figure 7–9 can point out where excessive inventory exists by warehouse. This overstocked merchandise can be transferred from one warehouse to another rather than entering a new manufacturing order. An accurate stock status report will highlight those stockkeeping items, ranges, or other components where action is required to reduce inventory.

A Management Inventory Control Report is displayed in Figure 7–10. This is a summary of the stock status or material purchasing reports. Figure 7–10 is for larger firms with computer applications. Smaller manual operations may use a format similar to Figure 7–11.

Management Inventory Control

An important guide is "inventory efficiency." This is the amount of inventory available to serve incoming customer orders. Managers often exclaim with alarm that, "We have two million units of inventory. Yet, we are not delivering the merchandise. WHY?"

Much inventory may exist in the pipeline; yet, substantial quantities may be assigned to orders and unavailable for shipment. Likewise, much of it may be discontinued, obsolete, and off-quality stock which lowers the efficiency of the inventory for serving incoming customer orders. Inventory efficiency is defined as:

$$\frac{\text{Inventory}}{\text{Efficiency}} = \frac{\left(\begin{array}{c}\text{Total Inventory} - \text{Overstock} - \text{Discontinued} \\ \text{or Obsolete} - \text{Off-quality} - \text{Assigned to Orders}\end{array}\right)}{\text{Total Inventory}} \times 100$$

An example of the inventory calculation for the first week in Figure 7–11 is:

$$\text{Inventory Efficiency} = \frac{2,000 - 600 - 500 - 0 - 100}{2,000} \times 100 = 40\%.$$

The key element is maintaining control of merchandise "assigned to customer orders." It is in this category that strict control must be maintained to

FIGURE 7-9

Stock Status and Material Purchasing

Week Ending: xx/xx/xx

Model and Color	Total Inventory	Assigned to Customer Orders	Discontinued and Obsolete	Inventory over 3 Months	Warehouse Inventory Available	Forecast 1 Month	Forecast 3 Months	Replacement Orders in-Process	Order Priority	Week of Inventory	Over-stocked	Inventory Efficiency
Perculator—10-Cup												
Black	800	100	200	0	700	300	900	0	2.7	12	0	62
Silver	100	0	50	0	100	200	600	500	0.5	2	0	50
Beige	400	0	50	250	400	50	150	0	0.0	33	250	25
Total	1,300	100	300	250	1,200	550	1,650	500	—	10	250	50

FIGURE 7-10

Management Inventory Control

Date: xx/xx/xx   Warehouse: Dallas

Model No: 1740 Name: Colonial

Color	Width	Total Finished Inventory	Assign to Orders	In Transit	Back Orders	Future Orders	Memo Future Orders	Net Available Inventory	Percent Inventory Efficiency	Minimum Inventory	Maximum Inventory	Over-(Under-)stock	Average Wkly. Estimated Sales	Weeks Inventory	Turns
10	12	325						325	50	120	165	160	32	10	5.1
20	12	120						120	100	284	576	(164)	108	1	46.8
30	12	881						881	55	225	486	395	97	9	5.7
40	12	844						844	22	126	188	656	23	37	1.4
50	12				241			241–	100	256	504	(497)	92		.0
60	12	685						685	100	791	1,614	(106)	305	2	23.1
70	12	572	120					452	100	942	1,212	(490)	100	6	9.1
Total		3,427	120		241			3,066	64	2,744	4,745	1,211 (1,257)	757	5	

FIGURE 7-11

Management Control Report

Week Ending: 3/30/xx

(Units: 000)

Week Ending	Total Inventory	Assigned to Customer Orders	Discontinued and Obsolete	Inventory over 3 Months	Warehouse Inventory Available	Forecast		Orders Placed or Required	Week of Inventory	Over-stocked	Inventory Efficiency
						1 Month	3 Months				
4/ 6/xx	2,000	100	500	600	1,800	550	1,650	0	16	600	40
4/13/xx	1,500	200	400	400	1,300	600	1,900	300	10	400	33
4/20/xx	1,800	400	100	250	900	650	1,500	500	12	100	67

insure that orders on the books are real and will be shipped. Merchandise must not be assigned to specific customers for long intervals when shipment is being delayed either at the customer's request, for credit approval, or other reason. Another opportunity for improving inventory efficiency is minimizing the amount of discontinued or obsolete or off-quality material held in the warehouse or at production points.

By building "inventory efficiency" into the management inventory control system, managers can follow this statistic and significantly improve the quality of inventory available to serve incoming orders. Emphasis can be placed on customer service to reduce the quantity of merchandise assigned to orders and merchandise held for customers who may be delaying shipment in an effort to reduce their own inventories. In-transit merchandise can be expedited and inefficient inventory (discontinued, obsolete, off-quality, overstocked, and assigned to orders) can be reduced.

Up to this point, methods of control reports for operations have been displayed and explained. Executive management cannot concern itself with all the details of individual stockkeeping items, regional warehouses, or production planning by plant.

Top Management Inventory Control

Managers do need a control report by major item, region, plant, or total. This report should show management what inventory should be, where troublesome conditions exist, and aid them in asking the true and important questions. Such a report is listed in Figure 7–12.

This report shows the units as well as monetary value. The planned units are based on specific definable factors—lead times, service levels, and management prerogatives. The planned inventory is calculated. It is not based on inventory turns or other nebulous determinations.

Overstocked and understocked conditions are listed. Many reports list overstocked or other excess stock areas. For managers wishing to serve customers, understocked is equally important. The service levels (both standard and actual) are contained in this report. Also included is a summary of discontinued, obsolete, off-quality, or other merchandise which lowers the quality of inventory throughout the system.

In addition to knowing the inventory control at a specific point in time, managers must have consolidated reports which show trends or changes in trends. The summary report by week in Figure 7–12 could point up areas requiring management attention. Such a report for small operations or outlying warehouses was previously displayed in Figure 7–11.

A key opportunity for management to reduce inventories in the system is through the elimination of slow-moving items and unnecessary outlying distribution points. An example of four different sales levels and safety stocks required to maintain service is illustrated in Figure 7–13. Item 1 has a sales volume of 30 units. Because of this low volume, any incoming order of a reasonable magnitude will generate an out-of-stock condition unless a large

FIGURE 7-12

Management Finished Goods and In-Process Inventory Control Report

Date: xx/xx/xx

Model	Capacity	Color	Planned Inventory		Actual Inventory		Overstocked		Understocked		Service Level		Control
			Units	Amount	Units	Amount	Units	Amount	Units	Amount	Standard	Actual	
1022	6	Black	887	$ 3,548	1,040	$4,160					95	85	—
1022	8	Brown	400	1,600	920	3,680	470	$1,880			95	100	Overstocked
1022	10	Beige	3,389	10,167	3,000	9,000	0	0	198	$594	95	90	Understocked
1022	12	Gold	1,052	5,260	1,808	9,040	0	0	0	0	95	91	—
Off-quality													
Discontinued													
Total inventory			xx,xxx	xxx,xxx	xx,xxx	xxx,xxx	x,xxx	xx,xxx	x,xxx	xx,xxx	xx	xxx	

FIGURE 7–13

Sales Volume and Safety Stock Requirements

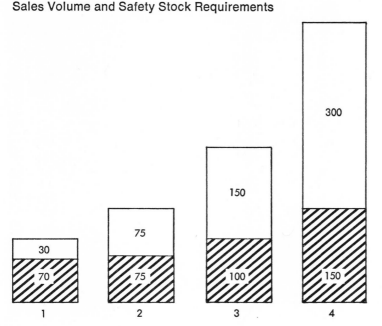

safety stock (70 units) relative to sales volume (30 units) is maintained. The reverse situation occurs with Item 4 where a large sales volume requires a relatively smaller safety stock. A similar situation exists in outlying warehouses, both in number of warehouses and stockkeeping items maintained in these warehouses.

Production Planning

Stock status and production planning reports by plant, component, module, or other segment can be organized as indicated in Figure 7–14. These utilize the forecasts, the inventory ordering, and management control for outlying and consolidated distribution points.

This report sums the production planning requirements for the entire inventory system. The total finished goods for the system, total assigned to orders, and total in-transit are listed. Back orders (those with delivery dates which are past due) are listed. These can be separated by regular orders, promotional requirements ("P"), contract or make-to-stock ("S"), or other breakdowns required. Future orders can be defined in a similar manner. The warehouse demand can be shown as a separate column.

This leaves the "available inventory" in the system. Work-in-process can be added to arrive at a "total available inventory." The reorder point and production lead time requirements can be calculated based on service level, forecast errors, lead times, and production, or other factors. The production

FIGURE 7-14

Stock Status and Production Planning Report

Date: xx/xx/xx

Model	Color	Size	Units Finished to Inventory	Assigned to Orders	In Transit	Back Orders	Future Orders Included	Future Orders Not Included	Warehouse Demand	Available Inventory	Work In-process	Total Available Inventory	Production Reorder Point	Production Lead Time Demand	Production Required Units	Priority
3660	3740	12	5,122	2,686		600 P / __600__	800 / 1,500 P / __2,300__	400 / __400__		464–	478	14	4,701	9,461	9,447	A0.00+
Total															__9,447__	
3660	4770	12	9,550	1,455		200 / 600 P / __800__	700 / 2,300 P / 200 S / __3,200__	100 / __100__	800 B / 100 C / 2,100 M / __3,000__	1,095	537	1,632	8,067	17,162	15,530	A0.20+
Total															__15,530__	
3660	4800	12	7,523	100			100 / 300 P / __400__	100 / __100__	3,000	7,023		7,023	1,516	2,570		C4.29+
Total																
3660	2700	12	13,066	2,608		600 P / __600__	300 / 2,500 P / __2,800__	200 / __200__		7,058		7,058	4,245	8,835		B1.66+
Total						__600__	__2,800__	__200__		7,058						

required can be compared with the manufacturing orders in process to determine whether or not additional manufacturing orders should be placed through the system. In this example, the mathematical requirements are calculated for "manufacturing orders." These must be rounded off to economical manufacturing units or economic order quantities.

An important statistic is "priority." Priority is:

$$\text{Priority} = \frac{\text{Total Available Inventory}}{\text{Production Reorder Point}}$$

A negative (minus) priority points to a back order situation. A positive priority up to 1.00 indicates production required within the normal lead times. A priority in excess of 1.00 shows those items which will be required at a subsequent time.

In scheduling production, it can be planned to produce the lowest negative priority first. This will insure that the oldest customer orders are served with the initial production batch. Then, production can be scheduled in sequence as required.

Where idle capacity exists, the lowest positive priority can be scheduled which permits production planning to schedule the particular production which is most likely to be required on subsequent reports.

Utilizing a system of priority brings discipline to the manufacturing function. Manufacturing managers like to make the longest production run practical. Manufacturing supervisors can schedule that production which will give them the best operating cost. The need is to service customers. A priority system is a good way to insure that customer service is balanced with manufacturing requirements.

CUSTOMER SERVICE

Good inventory control requires discipline in the sales force and customer service areas.

Customer service rules are required to insure that merchandise is assigned to the orders most likely to be shipped. Orders must always be carefully controlled to insure that customers are not ordering merchandise, having it assigned to their order, and then leaving it in the firm's warehouse. Customer service personnel must monitor orders to insure shipment.

As an example, assume that a customer orders 100 units of a particular item for shipment two weeks in advance. Suppose, then, the customer requests a delayed shipment. The merchandise should be removed from assignment, assigned to an order which will be shipped, or put on a free-for-sale basis. The customer should be advised that the merchandise will be assigned to his order again when shipping instructions are firm. Converting inventories to money is essential to improve short-term financial results.

Operating personnel sometimes like to insure that merchandise will be available to serve customers. They do not like to be rescheduling, to spend too much time expediting, or following up. Many production planning and customer service systems permit personnel to build too much security and thereby cause excessive inventories.

Managers must always determine the factors which affect inventories. The key one is lead time in supplying merchandise to outlying warehouses or in manufacturing. By cutting down the lead time, inventories can be reduced by an important amount. It is in this situation that real time on-line computers can be an important asset.

As an example, if the normal demand is 1,000 units per week and one week of lead time can be taken out of the system, approximately 500 units of inventory can be eliminated without reducing customer service. Lead time includes paperwork handling, manufacturing scheduling, processing, and transportation to warehouses or customers. Reduction in lead times is an opportunity to reduce inventory and improve short-term financial results.

Forecast accuracy can reduce inventories. The safety stock required to provide a particular service level is related to the accuracy of the forecast. Therefore, improving forecast accuracy can maintain the same customer service with fewer inventories.

The customer service level desired influences the inventory in the system. Is a high service level necessary? Service level is the quantity of customer orders serviced within the time requested by the customer. Many marketing and sales managers like to have a very high service level—say, assign or ship 90 percent of the incoming orders for a day from available inventory. Yet, is this service level actually needed? In many cases, reliability of customer service is more important than instantaneous delivery. Given that a customer has been promised delivery on a particular date, the firm's reliability to meet this promised date may be more important than a high service level for incoming orders.

Delivering complete orders is another factor in customer satisfaction, as contrasted with instantaneous incomplete delivery. If six items are required by a customer to complete a project, it is a problem if five of these can be delivered instantly, leaving one for delayed delivery. This prevents the entire project from being completed. A similar situation exists when the six items are required at a particular location. Then, if the items are shipped on separate trucks, location and assembly difficulties will result.

For a company with limited working capital resources, it may be necessary to adjust inventories. Orders may be cycled and customer service levels assigned based on return on investment for each product or group of products (Chapter Six, Product Tiers). Managers can evaluate the profitability or contribution as equated with the capital required for inventory. Service levels and inventories can be adjusted accordingly. The important point is to know what minimum payback is required on a given product in order to justify or support the inventory.

Managers should:

Review and realign the firm's organization (Chapter Two) to more precisely define responsibility for inventory control.

Evaluate the product line (Chapter Three) and other characteristics of the business to reduce complexity in transactions.

Study the existing short-term sales forecasting systems, revise or modify these to improve accuracy for production planning and inventory control.

Study new product introductions and arrive at an improved forecasting method for new items. They should increase the sales per stockkeeping item.

Minimize the use of "inventory turns" and replace this guide with planned inventory targets based on the cause of inventories.

Institute management inventory control reports to permit managers to follow inventories more precisely. Specifically, they should develop the indicator of "inventory efficiency."

Utilize a production planning system bringing together the total inventory in the system as scheduled by "priority."

Investigate credit control procedures to insure that orders are not being "held for credit" excessively which distorts forecasts by stockkeeping item.

Reduce the number of slow-moving items in the product line or consolidate storage and shipment of slow-moving items in a centralized warehouse.

Investigate the possibility of discontinuing outlying warehouses or reducing distribution points through faster physical movement of merchandise from central warehouses to the customer.

SUMMARY

Inventory control is one of the best opportunities to improve short-term financial management.

The first step is organizing for effectiveness. The second step is reducing complexity—simplifying all products, transactions, processes, and outlying distribution points. These are areas of management decision rather than mechanical aspects of the system.

The real need for managers is to know economic expectations and changes in market conditions in the next 12 to 18 months. This can best be done with exponential smoothing, diffusion indexes, studies of consumer confidence, and tracking of the business cycles. Economic analysis is sometimes more predictable from psychology—the response of people to events and conditions—rather than from data and statistics.

More complex, mathematical, and computerized systems which do not significantly improve accuracy and reduce understanding are questionable.

Expensive econometric or business models which do not contribute to

RECOMMENDATIONS TO IMPROVE SHORT-TERM FINANCIAL MANAGEMENT

short-term results should be avoided. Diffusion indexes are an opportunity to improve forecasting techniques in the short term. Autocorrelation is a mathematical method of more precisely determining the replacement cycle in estimating the potential demand for replacement business.

Accurate forecasting of new business is a way to reduce inventories and diminish the potential for discontinued or obsolete losses. New product curves and other methods bring an element of discipline to new product introductions plus aid in reducing potential losses.

"Inventory turns" can be helpful, although as the only guide to inventory control, "inventory turns" are inadequate. This guide must be replaced with a "planned inventory" in units and monetary values based on the causes of inventory—service level, lead times, forecast error, and related factors. An important new guide for inventory control explained in this chapter is "inventory efficiency." Even with management decisions and adequate systems, customer service discipline is required to maintain control of inventories. Rules must be set up and followed to prevent customers from ordering excess merchandise and then cancelling the order or delaying shipment.

Improved financial results in the short term and expanded return on capital employed can be achieved by superior managers with improved inventory managment. A systematic basis using the best available statistical methods and data processing tools is needed to schedule production, control inventory, and provide management with the right information to make correct decisions.

chapter EIGHT

Profit Improvement

Cost control is not a department or function. It is a philosophy, a way of life from the factory floor to the executive suite of the superior firm.

Reducing Cost of Operations—Now!

FOUR STEPS to poor financial results begin with:

1. Complicated, heavy infrastructure and organization—centralized corporate offices—not geared to the actual needs of the business which afford heavy cost burdens on financial results.
2. Centralized, rigid, nonresponsive computer installations which are ineffective and fail to give management flexibility.
3. High interest costs from inadequately financed operations which deteriorate financial results and reduce cost competitiveness (Chapter Ten).
4. Company-owned aircraft to serve the ego of executives where no acceptable need exists.

For a business in crisis, managers should examine all long-range expenses for potential elimination in the critical short range. This is necessary even if certain expenses must be added back in future years.

SYSTEMATIC COST REDUCTION

A systematic cost reduction program based on engineered standards (Chapter Four) and cost control reports (Chapter Five) is the foundation for improving profits—*now!* These chapters covered the variable manufacturing expenses of utilities, supply costs, and similar expenses. This chapter concentrates on fixed and larger expenses including those normally overlooked—distribution, sales, advertising and promotion, and administration.

Many motivational programs exist to generate enthusiasm and cooperation with employees at all levels, and these are good. However, they are not a substitute for a methodical approach to cost reduction. Terms such as "PIP" or Profit Improvement Programs have a value, but these tend to build up into peaks which decline into a pervasive lack of interest, attention, or results. Managers may as well be straightforward and say cost reduction rather than hang on to cliches.

The first step in systematic cost reduction is to develop a list by department, expense account, or person of potential opportunities for cost im-

FIGURE 8-1

Cost Reduction Worksheet

Department: Fabrication		Fabrication Date: xx/xx/xx			Prepared By: James Jones	
Problem	*Factors Affecting Cost*	*Correction*	*Responsible Person*	*Target Date*	*Potential Savings*	*Follow-up*
Excess waste of flat steel	1. Base design requires a size which is not standard from steel suppliers.	1. Redesign base to use standard size.	Engineering Manager			
		2. Redesign base to use a standard size sheet which can be cut internally into multiple units with reduced waste.	Engineering Manager and Purchasing Manager			
		3. Purchase and maintain stock of standard size sheets in larger quantities.	Purchasing Manager			
	2. Faulty measurements in fabrication and incorrect drilling of holes.	1. Improve training of new operators.	Fabrication Manager			
		2. Develop jigs to aid drilling and eliminate unnecessary measurements.	Fabrication Manager			

provement. Then, each of these should be detailed as in Figure 8–1. Each opportunity for cost reduction is listed; the factors affecting costs are specified; and the correction needed is determined. A specific person is assigned the responsibility for achieving a specified target date coupled with potential savings and follow-up.

Very frequently a problem exists in one department which requires help from other areas to solve. The Figure 8–1 example is for a machine shop. Here, the steel waste is excessive. The Fabrication Department must build equipment to specifications and designs of the Engineering Department. The Purchasing Department purchases the sheet steel. Unless the Engineering Department designs its equipment to permit the utilization of standard sizes and shapes, the Purchasing Department is forced into purchasing non-standard items at a higher cost. If sizes are purchased which prevent the economical cutting of the base steel, the Fabrication Department cannot avoid waste. Therefore, a coordinated effort is required to reduce steel waste and cut costs.

This particular example involves potential savings in materials. Reducing material costs is a universal opportunity for almost every business. In addition to raw materials, there are in-process materials, equipment supplies, and packaging materials (Chapter Five).

The search for cost reduction should begin by separating out those items where immediate results can be obtained without endangering the long-run future of the firm. In general, the extremes—the large costs, the items where a small change will have a significant result—are those where attention should be concentrated. This includes fixed as well as variable expenses. Many costs can be reduced with little or no long-range impact on the business. These areas include the clerical staff (combination of jobs such as a secretarial group, rather than individual secretaries), branch warehouses, company aircraft, data processing, and others.

An overlooked opportunity for cost reduction is in-process and finished goods packaging. Escalation of prices has distorted the advantages and costs of some synthetic packaging supplies. Wasteful, disposable practices must be reversed. Economical, reuseable, and reclaimable containers can reduce the cost of wrapping, packaging, and in-process items. A simple item—like tape, as an example—when used in large quantities can result in substantial costs savings. This question needs to be asked, "How much tape is functionally required for proper packaging?"

It is always necessary to separate the true and important expenses which are necessary from the true and trivial ones which can be eliminated with little risk. As an example, a firm may have developed an image of high quality and excellence over the years. A lowering of the quality standards—in materials purchased, in in-process control, or in finished products—could reduce personnel and costs. This would be a wrong move, for it would be endangering the basic foundation and market image.

Another situation might involve a firm which has low cost and efficient operations. It might seem that the addition of engineers, computers, and other technicians could improve performance. Before any costs are added, it must be verified that real improvement in operations will occur. Otherwise, these added costs will reduce the financial results in the short term and the character of the firm in the long term.

All changes must be carefully thought out in advance. The more fundamental the change involved, the more time and detailed evaluations are needed. A good idea today will be a good one tomorrow. Should a firm be in good financial condition, too many changes too quickly, whether in the interest of cost reduction or as a result of changes in the executive suite, can be detrimental.

Here are some specific opportunities for reducing costs of operations—*now!*

CORPORATE OFFICE EXPENSES

The creation of large, centralized corporate offices is not the way to build cost effectiveness or to improve management of the business.

Certain corporate expenses are essential. These include financial control, capital expenditures, legal, and top management policy setting. The creation of functions such as industrial engineering, data processing, corporate marketing and others at top level is questionable. There is always a need for coordination of these areas. There is not a need for large staffs.

To send out a team of transportation experts from corporate headquarters to a division to show them how to run their trucking operations, or to send a group of industrial engineers out to reduce costs, means that management in the division has abdicated its function. It implies poor management. Being constantly bombarded with the need to talk to and work with people from corporate offices diverts management at the division level from its prime task. Further, excess corporate involvement in division activities delays decision making. It tends to stymie management initiative. Good managers simply will not use their time talking to experts from the corporate headquarters. Either they will leave the firm or become politicians in the corporate structure.

Corporate expenses allocated to divisions can be a serious handicap in cost reduction. The arbitrary allocation or assignment of cost for which a division has no control will take much away from the enthusiasm of division managers to reduce their own costs. In the plant manager's mind there is nothing much to gain by eliminating two or three production workers when his plant is assigned a large corporate expense. It is meaningless to request a division to eliminate some clerical help when the executive force at the corporate level is loaded with salaries. As much profit improvement can be obtained by the elimination of one executive as by the termination of several clerks or factory employees.

If corporate expenses exceed one-half of 1 percent of sales volume, the firm begins to move from the superior classification to the average at 1 percent.

Above those levels, corporate costs become an intolerable burden which cannot be passed on to the customer in the market.

An example of corporate expenses for a firm with about $50 million in sales is illustrated in Figure 8–2. Corporate costs of $2,050,000 were nearly 4 percent of total sales. The firm was marginal and breaking even in good market conditions. With poor market situations, the firm went into a loss position.

New management reorganized and strengthened the divisions. Corporate surpluses and deadwood were eliminated. Corporate expenses were revised

FIGURE 8–2

Effect of Corporate Decentralization

	Division 1	Division 2	Total
Corporate Expenses for 12 Months Ending xx/xx/xx			
Finance	$ 210	$130	$ 340
Data processing	190	200	390
Engineering	60	20	80
Executive	270	290	560
Legal and corporate secretary	50	50	100
Industrial relations	190	100	290
Corporate marketing	60	90	150
Profit sharing	70	30	100
Contributions	20	20	40
Total	$1,120	$930	$2,050
Revised Corporate Expenses for 12 Months Ending xx/xx/xx			
Finance	$ 180	$180	$ 360
Legal and corporate secretary	15	15	30
Executive	210	210	420
Profit sharing	50	50	100
Total	$ 455	$455	$ 910

to $910,000. It is true that the full difference was not a reduction. About $400,000 (including some data processing) was transferred back to the division level. This left a net gain of $700,000 in short-term financial results without deteriorating performance or risking the long-term future of the firm. This $700,000 was all profit!

The elimination of unnecessary functions whether in the plant, in the office, at a division, or at the corporate level is an excellent opportunity to improve short-term financial management.

These reductions should be planned and managed on expense-by-expense and department-by-department bases. In times of declining profit, a directive may be issued by the top executive to reduce personnel by some arbitrary percentage, say, 10 percent. In many cases, this is an indication of poor management. The situation should never have occurred in the first place. Such arbitrary and overall edicts penalize the good department manager or responsible executive who has maintained excellent control of his cost.

Automated data processing can be one of the most useful, effective, and efficient functions in the business operation. It is a way to obtain more information on a timely basis to make decisions and take actions. It provides the opportunity to handle transactions with lower cost and higher sales volume without adding personnel.

Data processing is a department created to provide service or it should be eliminated. It is no black box technique within which mysteries are taking place. If it does not add value to the product which can be recovered in the market, expenses incurred by this department can be a heavy burden.

Industry has been working under the illusion for some years that data processing costs should be approximately 1 percent of sales. This is ridiculous. With 1 percent to corporate aircraft, 1 percent for corporate offices, 1 percent for data processing, and so on, there simply are not enough "percents" to go around and still earn a decent profit.

The cause or need for data processing is directly related to the transactions and essential information to operate the business. It is not related to any percentage of sales, to what can be done with the equipment, or to output information. As defined earlier, effectiveness is determining what should be done, while efficiency is doing a good job on a task. The first step relative to data processing is asking the question, "What should be done?"

An example of a cost reduction achieved by a firm is indicated in Figure 8–3. A large volume, high capacity computer was installed. Computer personnel were insensitive to division requirements and rigid in demands. Excess personnel were being carried to cope with unnecessary demands. Programs were inefficiently utilized. Equipment was leased from the computer manufacturer.

FIGURE 8–3

Cost Reduction in Data Processing Expense

	Cost per Month
Initial data processing cost	=$ 34,000
Reductions	
Computer II	$ 11,000
Division II terminal	1,000
Division II—peripheral equipment and terminal	1,000
Division II—telephone lines	1,500
Division II—plant 1, personnel	3,000
Division I—Plant 1, peripheral equipment and terminal	1,500
Division I—telephone lines	1,500
SubTotal: Reductions	−$ 20,500
Additions	
Additions—Computer I	$ 5,000
Maintenance on Computer I	1,000
Personnel.:	1,000
SubTotal: Additions	+$ 7,000
Revised data processing cost per month	$ 20,500
Savings per month	$ 14,000
Savings per year	$158,000

In order to reduce costs, the firm reorganized the data processing operations. A lower-cost computer and one with less capacity was quite capable of handling the needed functions. Leasing a machine from a firm which was not the original equipment manufacturer proved advantageous.

Programs were rewritten to reduce data storage and running time. The organization was streamlined and excessive reports were eliminated. Functions were transferred back to manual operations, rather than computer applications.

The result was a saving of $158,000 and greater efficiency. *Reducing automated data processing expenses is an excellent way to improve short-term financial results.*

There are cases where company aircraft are useful and effective, such as a situation where a plant is remotely located in relation to commercial operations. A chief executive with multiple divisions or senior executives can utilize their time more effectively when aircraft are available.

COMPANY VERSUS COMMERCIAL AIRCRAFT

Field service personnel repairing capital intensified equipment, responding to emergencies and like conditions can frequently use internal aircraft to an advantage. Potential customers can be brought to factories and sales conferences for professional selling.

In practically every case where company aircraft result in improved performance, multiple aircraft are required to insure availability of the type of aircraft to fit the need and to be ready when required. A firm is not acquiring a company aircraft, it is going into the aviation business. Because this requires specialized personnel, management should ask itself this true and important question, "Is going into the aviation business an essential activity for the firm?" Will entering the aviation business detract management from its primary business?" "Will a real return on the capital employed in the aviation business result?"

An estimated cost for operating a twin engine, turbo prop company-owned aircraft is displayed in Figure 8–4. This example assumes 50 hours of operation per month, or 600 hours per year. The utilization is assumed to be 90 percent which allows five-hours time per month for pilot training, testing, returning the aircraft to maintenance bases, or nonbusiness use. The speed is based on 375 miles per hour cruising speed with a 90 percent effectiveness. This reduction is to allow for delays on landing, slowdowns in traffic patterns, or other reasons.

The aircraft contains five seats at 375 miles per hour and 90 percent efficiency, or 1,688 seat miles per hour. The cost per seat mile with a full load of five people is $0.296. With an average load, it is $0.370. With one executive in the plane, the cost per seat mile becomes a startling $1.37.

At the time these figures were put together, the cost per seat mile for commercial aircraft after a multitude of fare increases resulting from the higher fuel cost was about $0.10 for economy travel, and $0.13 for first class.

FIGURE 8–4

Company-Owned Aircraft Cost

	Cost per Hour—50 Hours per Month
Depreciation	$ 100
Pilot	50
Copilot	30
Personnel expenses	25
Gas and oil	50
Repair and maintenance	35
Insurance	20
Miscellaneous: Hangar, rental, landing fees, etc.	15
SubTotal: Cost per hour	$ 325
Return on investment	$ 80
Target cost	$ 405
90 percent utilization	$ 450
Based on 375 MPH cruising speed 90 percent effectiveness	$ 500 per hour
5 Seats at 375 MPH ×90 percent effectiveness	1,688 seat miles per hour
Cost per seat mile Full load—5 people	$0.296
Cost per seat mile average load—4 people	$0.370

For commercial travel, there is no added expense for delays in landing resulting from flight conditions, weather, or other purposes. The cost relationship between company-owned and commercial aircraft travel costs remain valid even with changes which may take place from the assembly of these data.

There simply is no economic justification for a company-owned aircraft when commercial service exists on even a remotely accessible basis. Management's judgment on intangible factors is the basis for company-owned aircraft.

One way managers are misled is in aircraft utilization. The cost per hour comes down by flying more. How often are unnecessary trips generated simply to increase the flying hours?

The cost can be brought down by using a single pilot, rather than both a pilot and copilot. Further, the aircraft seating can be increased from five to six. The question becomes one of safety. Are managers willing to risk their people without access to a copilot in an emergency?

Managers must not overlook comfort. In most smaller planes, when fully loaded, the conditions may not be comfortable. They may not be useful for a working manager. In many cases, confidential matters need to be discussed. These cannot be discussed when the plane is filled with personnel whose access to this information is a liability.

In reporting operating costs and seat mile costs to managers, is the question ever asked, "Is this trip necessary?" A good way to test this is to arrange a flight by the company aircraft, then, ground the plane for a day or two. Do the people who were scheduled on the flight go commercial airline, or do they wait for the plane to be available? The plane may be scheduled to take one executive from point X to point Y. Then, every effort is made by the Aviation Department or person responsible to call around the office to see if anyone else needs to make the trip, just to fill the plane. The flight scheduling of the plane and encouraging of personnel to make unnecessary trips may reduce the calculated cost per seat mile or lower the estimated cost per hour by adding flying hours. But they do not save money!

The calculation of cost per hour includes a return on the capital employed (Figure 8–4). How many Aviation Departments, when calculating their cost per hour, include this very essential element? (In this example, the aircraft was assumed to have cost $420,000 with a $60,000 salvage value and six-year life.) Company aircraft should be analyzed, controlled, and return on investment obtained in a similar manner to that which is expected on a production piece of equipment.

These cost figures are based on propeller-driven aircraft. In many cases, a company-owned plane will do with great efficiency that which should not be done at all. (A jet aircraft will do with even greater efficiency that which is not needed.) They become a convenience rather than filling a need. When a downturn occurs, and it is necessary to reduce costs through elimination of executive aircraft, it is painful!

The best way to avoid the problem with company aircraft is never to acquire a company plane. If aircraft are needed, they can be obtained from chartered services which are reliable, certified, and safe. The type aircraft required for the occasion can be obtained. Customers can be brought to the factories and sales meetings with full conveniences—meals, hostess accommodations, and so forth.

The moral implications of company-owned planes cannot be ignored. Is it really fair for a small plane with only a few people to take the same air space, require the same approach in landing time, and utilize the identical equipment and control services of a jumbo jet transporting several hundred people?

A good way to improve financial results now is to eliminate aviation divisions. A good way to prevent losses in future years is not to have a company plane or company aviation business. A question management must ask is, "Will the acquisition of a company aircraft significantly improve performance?" The answer is generally, "NO."

COMPANY TRUCKS

Prompt and controlled distribution to the final customer is an element of completing the marketing concept. Company-owned trucks are a way to improve the reliability of deliveries.

Here, too, are some pitfalls for managers and opportunities to improve financial performance. When there are company trucks, how often are shipments delayed awaiting a full truck or batch? How much inventory is assigned to orders (Chapter Seven) awaiting the accumulation of a full truck to a particular location or customer?

The reports on the trucking operation generally reflect cost per mile of operation and cost per pound, unit, or cubic content moved. It may be that to obtain fully loaded trucks, the Trucking Division, in conjunction with the Shipping Department, is filling trucks with merchandise which may not be needed at the distribution center. There is much self-delusion about profits and costs in company trucking operations. This is particularly true when the operation is a corporate function with divisions being charged commercial carrier rates.

Internal trucking operations are sometimes justified on the basis of customer service. Yet, how frequently do our customers—large volume buyers, in particular—drive down profits by stating, "You have your own trucks. Give us the price f.o.b. our warehouse instead of f.o.b. your shipping point."

Internal trucking generally must have backhauls to break even or generate even a modest profit. If these backhauls are outside the control of the firm, the trucking operation can quickly develop into a loss in seasonal, cyclical, or other short-term economic slowdowns. These short-term losses can often more than offset any profits recovered over the longer term.

Many internal trucking units are based on leasing equipment. Management deludes itself that large percentage profits are obtained on little capital employed. A 100 percent return on a small investment is trivial. These leases tend to mislead managers into thinking the costs are variable. In fact, they are fixed and are a serious drain on profits and slow growth, cyclical economies.

Before beginning expensive trucking operations, the superior manager should ask himself, "Will the Trucking Division contribute significantly to reduced transportation costs and improved delivery?" If so, the personnel, organization, and equipment should be provided.

In many cases, the effective use of independent carriers eliminates the need for a Trucking Division. It is not enough for internal trucking operations to recover costs. These must also provide a return on the capital utilized by the Trucking Division.

COMPANY CARS

No greater abuse exists than in supplying company-owned vehicles to employees.

A company-owned car is not a fringe benefit. It is provided for business needs. It is bad management and it is illegal for an employee to utilize his company car and its expenses for personal activities.

The company car is certainly needed by salesmen and others; but what kind of company car is needed? The real need is for economical and safe transportation. A large, luxury car with high cost and excessive gas consumption is not needed. Company vehicles should be made available only to persons with a completely documented justification.

The elimination of company cars can be a right step in the direction of cost reduction. The reduction in the size of car and the utilization permitted can reduce expenses and comply with tax laws. Permitting company employees to use their company cars for personal activities is a tax loophole. Any use of the company car for personal activities should be considered income, gift, or salary. It is taxable and should reflect a saving to the company.

Affluent executives tend to be ego sensitive and status prone. The company car should not be a status symbol. The provision of company cars in excess of needs is a symbol of poor cost control.

Some sales managers justify a larger car as a necessity to entertain or impress customers. Customers would much prefer dealing with a low cost company, one that is not expending its money unnecessarily.

Membership at the local country club, in civic organizations, and in related activities is needed for customer entertainment and community relations. These, like company cars, are not fringe benefits. They are for a purpose, or they should be eliminated.

EXECUTIVE PRIVILEGES

How often does an executive take his wife, family, or friends to the country club for dinner at the company's expense? How often may a large group of company executives play golf with only a limited number of customers?

Country club membership and similar activities (normally considered executive privileges) can contribute dollars to the profit column by being eliminated.

The problem with any executive privilege, company car, or similar activity comes in a business slowdown. It may be that the company is making plenty of money and can afford to pay the cost. The tax on profits of the firm may be high and the net cost to the company might be lowered. Then, a downturn occurs or profits are eliminated. Executives have become accustomed to these privileges and become dissatisfied when these privileges have to be discontinued.

Executive privileges should be reduced to an absolute minimum. These expense items are too easily abused and become tax loopholes. Industry and management must discipline themselves or additional government controls will be placed over the free enterprise system to insure full tax collection and equity to public investors.

The trend to area-wide telephone service on a limited or continuous basis is a real asset to increasing sales, maintaining contact with customers, and improving business operations. The situation requires control and discipline to insure that these telephone services are meeting the requirements of the business.

TELEPHONE SERVICE

The cost of area-wide telephone service must be determined per minute. Assume a budget of $240,000 per year for these services. Then, allowing ten hours of usage per day, five days per week, and 48 weeks per year, the costs are:

Cost per year	$240,000.00
Cost per week—48 weeks	5,000.00
Cost per hour—50 hours per week	100.00
Cost per minute	1.67

The cost per minute becomes a startling $1.67 of planned usage.

How often are telephone calls made simply because the telephone service is available? Are area-wide telephones utilized to contact customers? Or are they primarily used by administrative personnel? Are they used by persons to call home on personal matters when traveling?

The training of customer service personnel to properly use telephones is essential to maximize these facilities. A random recording, with notification, can test the idle time of the telephone lines and determine whether abuses are occurring. Elimination of one nationwide line or its conversion to utilization by customers can improve sales or reduce costs.

Another opportunity to reduce telephone expense is by discontinuing unnecessary car telephones. In many businesses (construction, for example), vehicle telephones can be extremely important. In the case of business managers and executives, however, they may be unnecessary, costly, and a liability. (How often is confidential information, discussed over car telephones, picked up by other listeners?)

ADVERTISING AND SALES PROMOTION

It has often been stated that 50 percent of all advertising expenditures are wasted. The question is, which 50 percent?

The need for advertising and the type of advertising varies with almost every business and almost every country. Yet, every expenditure, every promotion, and every advertising campaign can be evaluated based on specific objectives, costs, and returns to the firm.

In general, funds must be utilized at the point of sale where the buying decision is finalized. For a major manufacturer with brand recognition nationwide, mass media advertising (television, major publications) may be justified. Even here, though, it must be limited.

Many products and manufacturers simply cannot afford these high priced media. When such advertising methods are utilized for minor products, they may influence a potential customer to come to a particular store for purchase of a product. When the customer arrives, the salesman may well sell him a competitor's product. In this situation, point-of-sale advertising is more effective than mass media.

Some advertising simply serves to inflate the ego of executives in the firm. These are advertising formats which show the person's photograph or other personal satisfaction technique.

Advertising and promotional expenses are especially vulnerable for cost reduction in the short term. For the firm in a crisis or a turnaround situation, funds which contribute to brand identification over the long run must be eliminated. The frequency of advertising and promotion, reduction of outside agency expenses, and elimination of personnel devoted to the creating of programs are excellent opportunities for cost reductions.

A professional approach to all advertising and sales promotion expenses on an analytical and objective basis is essential.

These are only a few of the potential accounts, costs, and expenses which offer an opportunity for reduction immediately without impairing effectiveness or long-term viability of the firm. There are other expenses which can be reduced. These include: trade associations, international travel, publications, professional services, trade shows, conventions, seminars, research and development, director's expenses, cost of annual report preparation, executive salaries, postage, and many others. **OTHER EXPENSE REDUCTIONS**

A systematic, methodical approach to cost reduction on an analytical and objective basis is essential. In Chapter Six, a Sales and Profit Forecast is put forth. The policy of constantly striving for added sales as a basis for higher profits is questioned. Throughout industry at home and abroad, a 1 percent cost reduction is equivalent to approximately 3 percent to 5 percent of higher sales volume. Cost reductions may not require higher inventories, accounts receivable, or other cash requirements to finance the higher sales volume.

Improving financial results in the short term requires a coordinated plan of action as follows:

1. Simplification of products and reduction of transactions (Chapter Three).
2. Engineering of cost calculations (Chapter Four).
3. Methodical approach to cost control (Chapter Five).
4. Control of pricing and improvement in the product mix (Chapter Six).
5. Reduction in inventories of raw materials, work-in-process, and finished goods (Chapter Seven).
6. Elimination of all expenses which do not contribute to higher sales and profits without excess risk to the long-term future of the firm (Chapter Eight).
7. Rationalization of the production process.

The first step in developing a plan to cope with a business slowdown is detecting the timing of the potential slowdown. Consider the conditions in the following example. **COPING WITH THE BUSINESS SLOWDOWN**

The firm has been very successful in a growing market. Sales increases have exceeded those of the industry average. Profits are running in excess of 10 percent on sales with 25 percent or more return on gross capital employed. New plant and equipment expenditures are pending, including larger staffs, data processing equipment, advertising, and others. **A Case Study**

Inventories are low in raw material, work-in-process, and finished goods. Raw materials, personnel, and energy are in short supply.

Yet, there are signs of a general slowing of sales or falling off in business. These include the following:

1. Studies of consumer confidence indicate a definite decline.
2. Interest costs remain high. Customers are asking for longer terms on purchases.
3. International developments and governmental news continue to depress public confidence.
4. Housing starts have been declining and are expected to continue to slow down.
5. Some shipments are being delayed, with goods assigned but not shipped, causing inventory increases.
6. The Credit Department's listing of past due accounts and potential bad debts has bottomed out and may be changing in trend upward.
7. Although orders and shipments remain good, there are indications that some of the items are being used to fill the pipeline and are hedges against shortages or price increases.

Clearly, these are indicators of a potential slowdown. How can a superior manager be prepared to cope with a fall-off in business? The areas of planning include maintaining sales, continuing the quality of accounts receivable, reducing costs, stretching out capital expenditures, reducing risks, and others.

Maintaining Sales

In each business or industry, there are ways of maintaining sales to be ready for a slowdown in the general market. These are listed below:

1. Step up advertising to help customers move inventory through the pipeline.
2. Devise special promotions—materials, products, and prices.
3. Consider strategically placed price reductions to increase sales and maintain volume through the factory.
4. Consider the advantage of larger quantity discounts or other financial incentives.
5. Improve installation, maintenance, and repair service to insure that customers will keep your product and not switch suppliers in a slowdown.
6. In products, prepare highly visible improvements in design, style, and quality.
7. Motivate the sales force and all management down to the supervisor level with short-term incentive opportunities.

And, there are others.

Maintaining sales volume is of no value unless payments are received for the merchandise. The sale is not complete until the cash is received. Cash collections and the quality of accounts receivable must be maintained (Chapter Ten).

What are some ways of achieving these objectives? Of necessity, some actions may even hurt sales volume in the short term.

1. Review the credit of each customer and his operations to determine how the customer's business will respond in a slowdown.
2. Encourage salesmen to help collect on sales to past due accounts.
3. Step up the timeliness of billing.
4. Follow up on past due accounts more quickly.
5. For marginal accounts, discontinue shipments or go on a cash-before-delivery basis.
6. Provide alternate credit sources to customers with questionable credit.
7. Improve the customer mix.

From a sales point of view, customers are generally ranked on a sales volume, profit, or contribution basis. These are excellent guides. A more systematic approach would be to develop a point system for evaluating customers as illustrated in Figure 8–5. This enables the ranking of customers on a variety of factors.

FIGURE 8–5

Basis of Retail Account Rating

Number and Sales Volume	Credit	Claims and Returns	Management	Growth	Profitability	Time Required
1. $50,000 or over ..	Excellent	Minimum	Excellent	Excellent	Excellent	Minimum
2. $40,000–$50,000..	Good	Average	Good	Good	Good	Average
3. $30,000–$40,000..	Average	High	Average	Average	Average	High
4. $20,000–$30,000..	Poor	Excessive	Poor	Poor	Poor	Excessive
5. $15,000–$20,000..						
6. $10,000–$15,000..						
7. $ 5,000–$10,000..						
8. Under –$ 5,000..						

The elimination of 10 percent to 20 percent of the customers who now require too much management time, demand too many claims and returns, and insist on excessive price reductions can improve short-term financial results. Those eliminated will make sales time available to obtain new accounts with better sales potential, management, and financial opportunities.

Cost Reduction

The opportunities for cost reduction are many. These have been covered earlier in this chapter and will not be detailed again in this case study.

Stretching Out Capital Expenditures

The key to return on investment on expanded facilities for capital expenditures is timing. Capital expenditures for added production and capacity should become available for production concurrent with business upturns.

Too often, managers and boards of directors are out of phase with reality in approving capital expenditures. When business and profits are good, expenditure justification and approval is relatively easy. In the low part of the cycle, managers are much more conservative.

The fact is that capital expenditures and expansions generally need to be started at a low point in the business cycle to be ready for the higher demands at a later time. In this case study, expansions are planned in plant and equipment, staffs, data processing equipment, and advertising expenditures. What actions could be taken to reduce the potential idle capacity losses of unnecessary productive facilities, the fixed cost losses of larger staffs, and data processing equipment?

1. Evaluate each and every capital expenditure—eliminate it, reduce it, or delay it until the proper time in the business cycle.
2. Eliminate or delay any additions to the staff.
3. Upgrade personnel and tighten discipline.
4. Upgrade the present plant and equipment to obtain higher productivity.
5. Reduce the product complexity and obtain higher productivity from existing plant, property, and equipment personnel.
6. Delay any decisions to expand marginal or service functions—data processing, and others.

Managing a business during a slowdown is the real test for superior managers. Even an average manager can earn money during a period of rising prosperity. The action managers take to survive a business slump generally make the manager and the company a better and sounder operation.

Every manager must be prepared to cope with the variety of business slowdowns which will occur. These include short-term seasonal decline within one year, cyclical business low points over a three- to five-year time span, fall-offs resulting from high technology over a period of one or more decades, long waves in the economic system, or worldwide political turmoil.

A well-managed company can hold its own or even continue to grow in the face of a business decline. This is the ultimate test of management's ability.

RECOMMENDATIONS TO IMPROVE SHORT-TERM FINANCIAL MANAGEMENT

Managers should:

Objectively analyze all corporate and central office expenses to determine those which can be eliminated.

Study data processing costs to find ways of reducing these expenditures while maintaining necessary functions.

Where company-owned aircraft are operated, consider the possibility of eliminating this activity and switching to commercial aircraft or charter facilities. In any event, a return on investment in aircraft must be demanded!

Review any internal trucking operations which may exist and investigate the cost of transferring to contract or commercial transportation. Also, insist on a return on investment in any funds expended for internal trucking.

Evaluate each company car, every executive privilege, telephone service, or other expense for potential reduction or elimination.

Consider eliminating in the short term advertising and promotion expenses associated with brand identification over the longer-range time interval, reduce the frequency of advertising activity, and cut back on internal personnel creating programs and external advertising agencies expenses.

Prepare a contingency plan and be ready for any business slowdown which may occur.

SUMMARY

A key opportunity to improve financial results in the short term is to eliminate or reduce those costs and expenses which do not contribute to sales and long-term growth. A systematic approach is required to insure that all potential cost reductions are detected and expenses eliminated. Motivational programs generate enthusiasm and these are good. However, a methodical and straight-forward approach to cost reduction is essential.

A typical cost reduction worksheet for reducing material costs is displayed in this chapter. The cost of raw materials, in-process materials, equipment supplies, and packaging is a universal opportunity for cost reduction.

Data processing and computer operations are excellent places to look for cost reductions. An example from the world of business on how a firm reduced its data processing expenses by $158,000 per year is included.

The elimination of company-owned aircraft is an excellent opportunity to reduce costs—NOW! An example is shown of the cost of company operated aircraft versus commercial or charter usage. Some pitfalls in the statistics reported to management on aircraft utilization are listed. Where aircraft are operated, management should insist on a return on investment in the funds expended for company aircraft in the same manner as it would for production equipment.

Company trucks, company cars, executive privileges, telephone service, advertising, and other typical expense reductions are suggested.

Managers must always be ready for a business slowdown. These can result within one year due to seasonal or other factors, in three- to five-year business cycles, in one or more decades of capacity saturation, or in long waves in the economy. A case study illustrates how to develop a contingency plan for coping with the business slowdown.

Large administrative offices, excessive data processing facilities, company-owned aircraft, and other similar expenses are indications of a potential decline in financial results. These are excellent opportunities to reduce costs and improve short-term financial management.

section four

Acquisition or Spin-Off
Money Management

chapter NINE

Acquisition or Spin-Off

It is not the company with the best facilities that achieves the most superior performance, or is the best acquisition candidate. It is the company with the best management team.

Acquiring a New Business or Disposing of One Which Does Not Perform Profitably

"IT TOOK me ten minutes and five million dollars to make the acquisition. Five years and ten million dollars later, we were out of it." And this statement with varying degrees of monetary values sums up the experience of many managers and acquisitions.

Acquisitions can be a very successful way to grow in sales and profits. These must be handled objectively and on an analytical basis. A successful acquisition requires systematic analysis of the firm. The terms of acquisition, financial factors, relationship to the existing business, and other factors must be studied.

The growth achieved by one firm through acquisitions coupled with expansion of existing businesses is illustrated in Figure 9–1. The firm's sales in the base year were about $200 million. Sales were tripled over a ten-year

FIGURE 9–1

Growth through Acquisitions

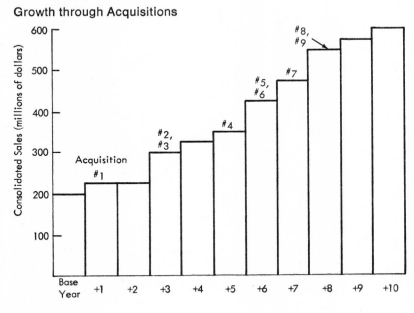

period to $600 million. Although some growth in this example was inflationary, the main impetus to higher sales and earnings was through acquiring other operations.

And profits did not suffer! Pretax earnings remained well above 10 percent of sales, approaching 15 percent in good years and 8 percent in the recessionary periods. Return on stockholder equity averaged 25 percent or more over the ten-year period. The firm's cash was not stretched beyond reasonable limits nor were excessive loans required to finance these acquisitions. Through professional tax management, and utilizing opportunities for increasing the tax depreciation base by expanding the asset values from historical cost to fair market value, the firm generated a substantial cash flow to finance acquisitions.

ACQUISITION ANALYSIS

Acquisitions must relate to the financial capability of the firm. Generally, acquisitions are a medium- or long-range opportunity. Sometimes the situation exists where a firm may have the financial resources for an acquisition even when it is performing marginally. One may be needed to enable increased sales, to offset idle capacity, and to improve cost competitiveness by internal manufacturing of a key part or component. In some situations, management talents could be acquired to strengthen the acquiring business. In most cases, the spin-off of an existing operation (page 172) has a higher priority in the short term than acquisitions.

The first step to successful acquisition analysis is to evaluate the need for an acquisition candidate. This must be done on a conceptual or judgmental basis prior to getting involved in negotiations or financial evaluations.

Planning Acquisition Strategy

A systematic approach to acquisitions is essential for success.

How does an acquisition of a manufacturing facility compare with construction of additional manufacturing capacity, if this is the need? Factors such as technological capability of the potential acquisition must be related to those which might be obtained with a new facility. The cost of an acquisition must be balanced against the losses in start-up costs of new construction.

How much training time is required for new personnel? How long will it take the new facility to break even? These and other questions must be considered in a methodical and organized manner.

Finding Acquisition Candidates

Before an acquisition candidate can be located, management should consider the acquisition criteria listed below.

Acquisition Criteria

1. Management
   a. What is the capability of current management? (Chapter Two, Figure 2–3).
   b. Would existing management remain with the firm?

     c. What is the potential for attracting new management?

     d. How is the firm organized, or will a reorganization be required? (Chapter Two).

     e. If the firm is managed by family members, how will they react if the business is not family-owned?

2. Product line.

     a. Are the products suitable for continued growth in sales, or are new products required? (Chapter Three).

     b. How do the firm's products compare with competition within the industry?

     c. Does the acquisition candidate have brand identification or other intangible assets?

     d. For the products of the firm, has the life cycle peaked? Is it growing or declining?

3. Sales and distribution

     a. Does the firm have broad sales and distribution?

     b. Are there opportunities for additional sales through trade channels and geographical areas which are not now served by the firm?

     c. Does the firm have a solid foundation of reliable customers capable of growth? (Chapter Eight, Figure 8–5).

     d. Have sales been achieved as a result of price cutting, or does a solid market program exist? (Chapter Six).

     e. Can the acquiring firm contribute to broaden the sales and distribution of the acquisition candidate?

4. Size of the firm

     a. What is the sales volume range desired for acquisition? (A firm must be careful to insure that an acquisition candidate is neither too large nor too small within the context of the existing business.)

5. Manufacturing capability

     a. What is the productive capacity of the manufacturing facilities?

     b. Does idle capacity exist from which higher sales could be obtained from existing assets?

     c. Is the technological capability of the firm equal to or better than that of competition?

6. Location of the firm

     a. What is the geographical location desired for an acquisition candidate? (A firm may have east coast facilities. An acquisition opportunity in the Midwest or on the west coast may be specified.)

     b. What is the availability of raw materials, personnel, and related resources?

7. Management control

     a. Has the firm maintained excellent control of its operations from a cost and efficiency point of view? (Chapter Four).

FIGURE 9-2

Point Evaluation of Acquisition Candidates

Company	Capability of Management	Continuity of Management	Location	Size and Capacity	Product Line	Brand Identification	Equipment Primary	Equipment Secondary	Sales and Distribution	Management and Control	Total Points
A.........	1	2	1	2	2	3	4	1	1	2	19
B.........	2	2	0	2	3	2	3	4	3	1	22
C.........	3	1	2	3	1	2	2	3	3	2	22
D.........	3	4	4	1	3	3	3	2	2	3	28
E.........	4	4	2	4	4	4	4	3	3	4	36
F.........	2	3	4	3	3	3	4	2	2	3	29
G.........	0	3	4	4	2	2	3	1	3	3	25
H.........	2	2	3	0	3	1	2	2	2	2	19
I.........	3	3	3	3	2	1	3	2	3	4	27
J.........	2	4	1	4	2	3	4	2	4	4	30
K.........	3	4	3	3	3	3	4	3	3	3	32
L.........	4	2	3	4	3	3	3	3	4	4	33

b. Are there opportunities for cost reductions to improve profits in the short term? (Chapter Eight).

c. Has good control been maintained of inventories—raw materials, work-in-process, and finished goods? (Chapter Seven).

These are examples of some of the questions and criteria for selecting potential acquisition candidates. In most cases, it is necessary to locate a business for acquisition. Those firms which are seeking to be acquired may not be the best candidates.

Then, once these criteria have been determined, potential firms can be sought and analyzed on a basis similar to Figure 9–2. The point values are assigned on the basis of:

Superior	4
Good	3
Average	2
Poor	1
Unacceptable	0

Admittedly, this involves judgment. It does force those evaluating acquisition candidates to think conceptually, to begin to ask the right questions, and to reconsider the acquisition criteria.

Once the companies have been listed in this manner, those for concentration can be sorted out based on the total points assigned. This type of evaluation need not be done by one person. It could be done by individuals within the firm and then their results compared.

For a firm which is acquiring a business outside its normal area, and when expertise on that business or its industry does not exist in the firm, it is always wise to have an evaluation made by outside consultants who are specialists within that industry.

Given the points assigned in Figure 9–2, the firms can be sorted for concentrated effort as listed in Figure 9–3. Given this analysis, efforts can be

FIGURE 9–3

Summary of Acquisition Candidates

Prospects	Company	Points	Explanation
Superior	E	36	
	L	33	
	K	32	
Good	J	30	
	D	28	
	F	27	
	I	27	
Average	C	22	
Poor and unacceptable	A	19	Management
	B	22	Location
	G	25	Management
	H	19	Size and capacity

concentrated on Companies E, L, and K, rather than scattered across a large group of companies in the industry or business.

Financial Projection

A key to any acquisition is its past performance in profits, return on capital employed, and cash flow. More important than the actual results for the past year is the trend. Has the potential acquisition candidate peaked or is additional expansion feasible?

A typical listing of financial results for an acquisition prospect is contained in Figure 9–4. All financial projections must be attacked in detail for possible errors. It is very easy for an acquisition prospect to put forth projections of increased sales and earnings with no valid basis or sound foundation to justify these results.

In the financial analysis, key determinations must be made in evaluating both current and fixed assets. Plant, property, and equipment fixed asset values can be reasonably determined by several methods. These include book value, current value, and replacement value. The book value can be obtained from the firm's tax reports. Current value and replacement value can be determined by competent persons or by outside evaluation firms.

The accounts receivable must be studied in detail. What is the real value? How many of the accounts will wind up as bad debts requiring adjustment in bad debt reserve?

FIGURE 9–4

Financial Results of Acquisition Prospect
(in thousands of dollars)

	Past Year	Projected Results		
		1st Year	2d Year	3d Year
Gross sales....................	$27,000	$30,000	$36,000	$40,000
Less discounts...............	2,000	2,200	2,600	2,900
Net sales.....................	$25,000	$27,800	$33,400	$37,100
Manufacturing expenses				
Materials...................	15,000	16,700	20,000	22,300
Personnel..................	1,100	1,300	1,500	1,700
Expenses...................	2,400	2,700	3,200	3,500
SubTotal:..................	$18,500	$20,700	$24,700	$27,500
Selling, general and administrative expenses				
Distribution.................	600	700	800	900
Sales and marketing..........	1,400	1,500	1,700	1,900
Administration..............	900	1,000	1,100	1,200
Financial expenses...........	400	500	600	700
SubTotal:..................	$ 3,300	$ 3,700	$ 4,200	$ 4,700
Total cost:....................	21,800	24,400	28,900	32,300
Profit before tax..............	3,200	3,400	4,500	4,900
Taxes......................	1,600	1,700	2,250	2,450
After tax profit...............	$ 1,600	$ 1,700	$ 2,250	$ 2,450
Depreciation................	700	800	1,000	1,100
Cash flow....................	$ 2,300	$ 2,500	$ 3,250	$ 3,550

Inventory is very frequently the biggest problem in determining asset value. It may sound simple to say, "Evaluate the inventory based on the lowest of costs or market." The problem comes in determining what costs *are* and what market value *is*. The acquisition prospect may have high cost operations and, therefore, overvalue its inventory.

What is the market value? This is extremely difficult to determine, particularly in industries where there are a large number of companies serving market needs with a wide variety of products. (Home furnishings would be a good example.)

How much of the inventory is discontinued, obsolete, or off-quality merchandise? Very close evaluation is required both physically and financially to insure that the acquirer is obtaining true value.

For a firm acquiring a business in an industry for which it already has an operation, it is easy to compare cost of the acquisition candidate prospect with those being attained internally. When the business is outside of the operating areas of the acquiring firm, it is a good idea to have cost comparisons prepared to determine the efficiency of the firm versus competition in that industry.

Many other financial factors would be involved including financing the acquisition, cash flow which might be obtained from operations, retrieving cash through disposal of assets of a prospect, and many others.

Tax Implications

The tax aspect of any acquisition is an extremely significant factor as it relates to the firm's existing operations and future considerations. A special study of tax advantages and disadvantages is necessary. These should be performed by competent professionals both within and outside the firm.

The ramifications of tax situations are so complex as to require special and detailed analysis outside the scope of this writing.

Terms of Acquisition

The terms of acquiring a firm involve much study and negotiation. The timing of the acquisition is an important factor in value determination.

The firm to be acquired may be in financial trouble and need cash to maintain sales growth. In this case, possibly taking over outstanding loans and debt coupled with small cash amounts might prove attractive.

Generally, firms looking for acquisitions shy away from those which are in financial trouble or those operating under court jurisdictions through bankruptcy proceedings. However, these firms may offer very attractive terms of acquisition. Facilities and markets may be obtained by simply taking over the management and guaranteeing the viability of accounts payable and loans after a given date.

The most important term of acquisition involves management and continuity of management. There is nothing to be gained by acquiring a firm with a successful management and then finding that these people leave upon acquisition. For owner-managers, the terms of acquisition could include an initial payment with a large portion of the acquisition price being paid over a five- or more year period based on operating performance. Other personnel need to be maintained on the management team with appropriate contracts, financial rewards, or other incentives.

Integrating the Acquisition into the Organization

Many of the best acquisition candidate prospects have entrepreneurial managers. These may have either started the business or taken it over at some point early in its development. Their drive, motivation to obtain financial rewards, and other factors could attain superior results.

Even with the best terms of payout, it is necessary to organize the acquisition into the acquiring firm successfully to maintain the initiative of the management within the acquired firm simultaneously with insuring control. The points covered in organization (Chapter Two) and expense control (Chapter Five) may be reviewed for this purpose.

Blending entrepreneurial managers into a corporate organization presents an extremely sensitive problem. For instance, a large firm using the proper tools of acquisition analysis may acquire a successful business. Nevertheless, the acquired firm's results slowly deteriorate. One of the prime reasons for this deterioration is a lack of knowledge by the corporate office or staff of the acquiring firm. In an effort to take over control, various specialists may be sent to the acquired firm. They may not know enough about its business to make intelligent suggestions. They may take up too much of management's time, causing deterioration in performance. The owner-managers may simply withdraw or fail to take the proper initiative as a result of so many "so-called" specialists—personnel, industrial engineering, financial, data processing—coming into the operations.

With the wide variety of people and conditions, both in acquiring firms and those being acquired, careful consideration must be given to insure that the acquired firm is allowed to operate in the environment in which it is most likely to be successful.

Deterioration of Existing Operations

A firm making an acquisition must be careful to insure that in so doing they do not permit existing operations to decline.

When an acquisition is finalized, managers handling the acquisition want it to be successful. Therefore, they frequently devote an undue amount of their time and attention to the acquired operation. Managers are distracted from existing operations. Performance in these businesses may deteriorate. Opportunities for improvement in the existing enterprise may be overlooked.

SPIN-OFF OF AN OPERATION

The elimination of an existing business, division, or factory manufacturing operation is a real opportunity to improve financial results and the viability of any business, particularly in the near future.

In every activity, there is some area, some department, or some unit which is not contributing. It may be this one area is pulling overall results down substantially.

For some reason (management ego, status, or desire not to face up to failure), most managers do not have the courage to dispose of poorly performing units. This is particularly true where the manager himself has been involved in the expansion or acquisition.

In the short term, it is easier to improve operations through disinvestment, disposal, or spin-off of an existing activity, than through acquisition. Here is a study of a situation, the actions taken, and the results of the firm's spinning-off a firm.

Case Study

The firm had several operating units of different businesses. Business I had two divisions: Division A and Division B.

These were geographical units with Division A in one location and Division B in another. Overexpansion occurred resulting in an excess of plant, property, and equipment. This was compounded with a cyclical slowdown causing reduced sales. Further, one of the manufacturing units could not expand or convert to more profitable products as a result of environmental protection restrictions.

Management prepared an analysis to determine if a step backward, disposal of one division, and reduced sales coupled with consolidation would improve operating performance.

Investment and Profit Analysis

An investment and profit analysis is listed in Figure 9–5. Phase I of the consolidated operation is one year later and Phase II is two years later.

FIGURE 9–5

Investment and Profit Analysis
(dollars in thousands)

	Business I			Consolidated Operations	
	Division A	Division B	Total	Phase I	Phase II
Sales units......................	5,400	3,000	8,400	6,000	8,000
Sales...........................	$16,200	$12,000	$28,200	$27,600	$36,000
Average selling price..............	3,000	4,000	3,357	4,600	4,500
Profit range					
Minimum.....................	(2,940)	(900)	(3,840)	800	2,300
Most likely....................	(910)	(700)	(1,610)	1,200	3,000
Maximum.....................	(90)	(400)	(490)	1,700	3,700
Total current assets..............	11,870	4,800	16,670	9,825	11,500
Net fixed assets..................	4,300	4,640	8,940	5,800	6,000
Total assets..................	16,170	9,440	25,610	15,625	17,500
Capital employed.................	13,275	8,200	21,445	12,425	15,000
Pretax.......................					
Return on capital employed					
Minimum.....................	—	—	—	6.4%	15.3%
Most likely....................	—	—	—	9.7%	20.0%
Maximum.....................	—	—	—	13.7%	24.7%

The range of profits is listed using techniques involving probability and uncertainty (Chapter Six, Figure 6–12 and Figure 6–13).

Clearly, in this situation with excess capacity and reduced sales, both Division A and Division B cannot be successful. Not only will financial results be improved by consolidation, but the capital employed would be reduced substantially. This would permit Business I to be placed on a sound financial foundation and to contribute cash to the corporate organization to improve liquidity.

Cash Employed Analysis

The cash employed detail is listed in Figure 9–6. In this situation, the cash employed is reduced over a one-year period from $21,445,000 to $12,425,000. In Phase II, cash employed must be increased. Yet, at this point in time, profits justify the additional cash input. Further, much of the additional cash required for Phase II is generated over the two-year period involved in Phase I and Phase II operations.

Such changes in cash employed did not occur by chance. Strict control of accounts receivable and customers being served was necessary to eliminate those few customers who were not paying their bills on time and generating

FIGURE 9–6

Cash Employed Analysis
(dollars in thousands)

	Business I			Consolidated Operations	
	Division A	Division B	Total	Phase I	Phase II
Sales—units....................	5,400	3,000	8,400	6,000	8,000
Sales..........................	$16,200	$12,000	$28,200	$27,600	$36,000
Accounts receivable..............	5,400	3,000	8,400	4,500	6,000
Inventories					
Raw materials..................	2,900	500	3,400	1,700	2,300
Work-in-process...............	350	100	450	800	1,000
Finished inventory.............	1,900	1,000	2,900	1,000	1,200
Supplies and other.............	250	100	350	225	300
Total inventories...............	$ 5,400	$ 1,700	$ 7,100	$ 3,725	$ 4,800
Other assets...................	900	100	1,000	400	700
Total current assets............	$11,700	$ 4,800	$16,500	$ 8,625	$11,500
Less accounts payable............	(2,725)	(1,330)	(4,055)	(2,000)	(2,500)
Net working capital............	8,975	3,470	12,445	6,625	9,000
Net fixed assets................	4,300	4,700	9,000	5,800	6,000
Total capital employed...........	$13,275	$ 8,170	$21,445	$12,425	$15,000
Key ratios per $1.00 sales					
Current assets..................	$0.72	$0.40	$0.59	$0.31	$0.32
Accounts receivable.............	0.33	0.25	0.30	0.16	0.17
Inventories...................	0.33	0.14	0.25	0.14	0.13
Other.......................	0.06	0.01	0.04	0.01	0.02
Total current assets...........	$0.72	$0.40	$0.59	$0.31	$0.32
Less accounts payable...........	0.17	0.11	0.14	0.07	0.07
Net working capital.............	$0.55	$0.29	$0.45	$0.24	$0.25
Sales Per $1.00 Fixed Assets					

the longest overdue accounts receivable. Simplified product planning (Chapter Three) reduced the complexity of products. This simplification and improved systems for inventory control (Chapter Seven) lowered inventories immensely. Cost reductions throughout the operations (Chapter Eight) improved costs including the corporate charges.

Managers often overlook the amount of cash required to grow in sales volume. As an example, Figure 9–6, based on the existing operations, shows $0.45 was required to finance each $1.00 of sales. With a revised operation, the cash required to finance $1.00 of sales was $0.25. Many businesses cannot finance their sales growth from existing operations. Some will move ahead to obtain sales growth at any cost. Through factoring, long- and short-term loans, the financial foundation (Chapter Ten) of the corporation or the business will be eroded. Therefore, it is often necessary for businesses to grow in sales volume for a two- or three-year period; then, hold sales volume level for one or two years to generate cash.

Cash Flow Analysis

A detailed analysis of the cash flow and cash flow return on capital employed for this case study is shown in Figure 9–7.

This analysis, particularly the cash flow on return on capital employed, demonstrates the necessity of taking the drastic action to eliminate Division A. There is simply little or no probability that success can be achieved in the short term by maintaining both divisions. Even if sales were available, the cash would probably not be available. The return on that cash would be highly marginal.

By consolidating and spinning-off Division A, there is a possibility within the probability limits that a minimum of 15 or a maximum of 20 percent cash flow can be obtained on the capital employed.

FIGURE 9–7

Cash Flow Analysis
(dollars in thousands)

	Business I			Consolidated Operations	
	Division A	Division B	Total	Phase I	Phase II
Depreciation.............	$ 900	$1,000	$1,900	$1,100	$1,100
Profit range				After Tax	
Minimum..............	(2,940)	(900)	(3,840)	400	1,150
Most likely.............	(910)	(700)	(1,610)	600	1,500
Maximum..............	(90)	(400)	(490)	850	1,900
Cash flow					
Minimum..............	(2,040)	100	(1,940)	1,500	2,250
Most likely.............	(10)	300	290	1,700	2,600
Maximum..............	810	600	1,410	1,950	3,000
Cash flow—return on capital employed					
Minimum..............	—	1.2%	—	12.1%	15.0%
Most likely.............	—	3.7%	1.4%	13.7%	17.3%
Maximum..............	6.1%	7.3%	6.6%	15.7%	20.0%

In this particular example, about a $1 million write-down in assets was required plus about $200,000 in close-out costs for Division A. Yet, this was offset by a pickup in book value through sale of the plant and property. Losses in the transitional period caused by write-down of inventory values, accounts receivable, and related assets actually increased cash flow. As a result of income taxes paid in earlier profitable years, a tax drawback resulted. This cash was used to reduce short-term debt, lower interest costs, and improve the financial base.

Superior performance in business requires careful management of existing operations, the constant seeking and evaluation of acquisitions, and the disposal of those which do not contribute. It is not enough for managers to look to existing operations to maintain the necessary growth in the business.

There is no such thing as maintaining a plateau of operations or sales volume. A business will either grow or decline. It will grow through acquisition and expansion of existing operations, or it will deteriorate through inactivity. Spinning-off existing operations is often necessary and essential, particularly for businesses in a crisis. A spin-off may be necessary for survival.

RECOMMENDATIONS TO IMPROVE SHORT-TERM FINANCIAL MANAGEMENT

Managers should:

Periodically evaluate the opportunity to achieve growth in sales and earnings through acquisitions.

Prepare a systematic, objective, and analytical evaluation of the various acquisition candidates available when acquisition has been deemed necessary.

Constantly study each business, each division, and each activity to determine when those activities which are not contributing should be eliminated.

SUMMARY

A successful way to grow in sales and profits is through acquisitions. These must be handled on an objective and analytical basis. A successful acquisition requires systematic analysis of a firm, its relation to the existing business, terms of acquisition to motivate management to continue excellent performance, and a thorough study of financial factors involved.

The first step is to plan the acquisition strategy. Then, the criteria for acquisition candidates must be prepared. A list of key points and questions which should be asked are listed in this chapter. The point method of evaluating certain key points about potential acquisition candidates (capability of management, size and capacity, product line, equipment, and so forth) is illustrated so that attention can be concentrated on those few acquisition candidates which will fill the predetermined criteria.

The importance of financial projections and pitfalls involved in analyzing financial data are discussed. On many reports to managers on potential acquisitions, the studies contain about 90 percent financial statistics and 10 percent evaluation. In fact, the opposite situation should exist.

Many potential acquisitions employ entrepreneurial managers. A prime task is to determine how to integrate the acquisition and its management into the acquiring firm. Careful consideration must be given to insure that the firm being acquired is allowed to operate in the environment in which it is most likely to be successful.

An important and intangible factor is the effect of an acquisition on existing operations. Management's attention must not be diverted from present operations which permits these to deteriorate.

In every activity, there is some area, some department, or some unit which is not contributing. It may be this one area which is pulling overall results down substantially. Elimination of existing business, division, or factory manufacturing operation is a real opportunity to improve the financial results and the viability of any business.

This chapter contains a case study showing the effect of disposing of one division of a business. Managers often overlook the need for cash to finance higher growth in sales. This typical example in the case study demonstrates how the cash required for $1.00 of sales was reduced from $0.45 to $0.25. Financial projections and cash flow analyses are illustrated, using probability ranges.

Superior performance in business requires careful management of existing operations, cautious acquisition, and the disposal of those divisions which do not contribute. It is not enough for managers to look to existing operations to maintain the necessary growth in the business.

To improve financial results, the marginal business or one in crisis may be forced to spin-off a plant, division, or subsidiary to survive a short-term liquidity crisis.

chapter TEN

Money Management

Too much interest on loans, too many leases on buildings and equipment, too much stretching of the available dollars, and too little cash flow reduces the flexibility of a business to respond or cope with a business slowdown.

Building a Sound Financial Foundation

"WHAT IS OUR BUSINESS?", "Who are our customers?", and "What are our resources?" Regardless of the answers to marketing and business questions, the job of managers is money management. *The one common foundation of successful business over the long run is sound financial management.*

Cash management is not the last chapter in this book because it is least important. It is last because it is influenced by management decisions and actions—acquisitions, cost control, product planning, inventory control, spin-offs, and others. Cash management is the most important of all!

CASH STRATEGY

The first step in cash management starts with a strategic approach to business.

A privately held business may wish to minimize profit, thereby reducing taxes and increasing cash flow through depreciation. Publicly held companies sometimes wish to maintain growth in profits per share simultaneously with cash flow.

The structure, trade channels, product philosophy, customer service, and related decisions must be considered in building a sound financial basis. A balance is needed to achieve a reasonable degree of financial security.

It is a good idea to draw a schematic diagram (Figure 10–1) illustrating the business and showing where the cash is used. By putting absolute amounts into a diagram of this type, it is possible to determine in which business funds are employed and where they are consumed. Using an overlay for each business, each division, or each method of distribution, it is possible to find cash-hungry parts of the enterprise.

It may be that much cash is tied up in plant and equipment to produce some materials, parts, or other items which could be purchased outside. This may give managers a clue to that portion of the business which should be spun-off (Chapter Nine) to build a sounder financial foundation now.

There is no one good method to make a sound decision on an investment. A balance is required between percentage of sales profits (or unit profit), return on capital employed, and competitive advantages which must be considered.

It is necessary to divide the capital utilized into fixed and variable categories. This is essential to cope with business slowdowns. The fixed capital needs to be minimized to protect the business in a downturn. This is a necessity even if higher short-term interest requirements retard profits in a growth situation.

An actual example of the change in the financial situation of one firm is listed in Figure 10–2. Year "X" was a business cycle peak, while year "X + 1"

FIGURE 10–1

Diagram of Cash Requirements

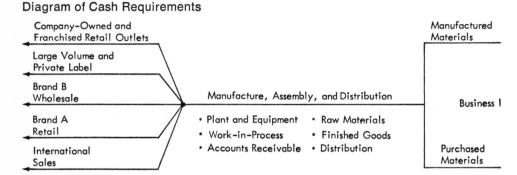

was a trough. In this case, sales declined and interest rates increased on both short- and long-term loans. The need to convert some loans from short- to long-term simultaneously with higher short-term interest rates boosted the financing cost fantastically.

In the Figure 10–2 example, the profit in year "X" was $4 million. A loss of $3 million occurred in year "X + 1." This shift of $8 million was the result of lower sales volume, higher cost of goods sold, larger loans, and much higher interest rates.

The firm was already underfinanced in year "X." The interest expense of $2 million on sales of $60 million was 3.33 percent. In year "X + 1," the financial cost approached 10 percent of sales. This occurred even with reductions in accounts receivable and inventories which more than doubled the reduction in sales.

When a firm's financing expenses exceed 1 percent to 2 percent (including interest, factoring charges, and related costs), the business is approaching a crisis in the event of a business slowdown. With normal profits before tax in a range of 8 to 12 percent, industry and business in general simply cannot afford, over the long term, the burden of excessive financial expenses. This is particularly true of fixed expenses where little cash flow is returned—leased equipment, long-term debts, and related types of financial resources. With high financial costs, managers' options to respond to a downtown or to take advantage of opportunities in an upturn are severely restricted.

It is necessary to plot the important aspects of business relative to competition to find those strengths which are important and those weaknesses which must be overcome. A conceptual chart is contained in Figure 10–3.

Internal raw material manufacturing may be excellent from a cost point of view. It may not be advantageous, however, if such investments increase the financial liability of the firm. A relatively high cost and low technology

FIGURE 10–2

Simplified Financial Data
(in millions of dollars)

	Year X	Year X + 1
Assets:		
Current assets:		
Cash.....................................	$ 1	$ 1
Accounts receivable......................	25	20
Inventories..............................	25	20
Subtotal..............................	$51	$41
Other assets:		
Plant and equipment—net................	20	21
Other.................................	4	3
Total.................................	$75	$65
Liabilities:		
Current liabilities:		
Loans—short-term.......................	20	25
Accounts payable.......................	15	12
Other.................................	5	3
Subtotal..............................	$40	$40
Other liabilities:		
Loans—long-term.......................	10	15
Stock and retained earnings..............	25	10
Total.................................	$75	$65
Profit and Loss:		
Sales...................................	60	54
Cost of goods sold.......................	44	42
Selling and marketing....................	4	4
General and administrative................	5	6
Net income from operations...............	$ 7	$ 2
Financial cost...........................	2	5
Gross profit or (loss)....................	$ 5	($ 3)

business can achieve good results with excellent products, superior management, and efficient distribution.

Market share is a component of success which can be overemphasized. Where a few manufacturers exist for a major market (automobiles), market share would require a higher relative value on the scale of points assigned in Figure 10–3. In most industries, where multiple sources of supply are available and no one firm has more than 10 percent to 20 percent of the market, market share may take a secondary position.

Where a firm has more than 10 percent market share, there does seem to be some correlation of profit and market share. With less than 20 percent to

FIGURE 10–3

Diagram of Strengths and Weaknesses Versus Competition

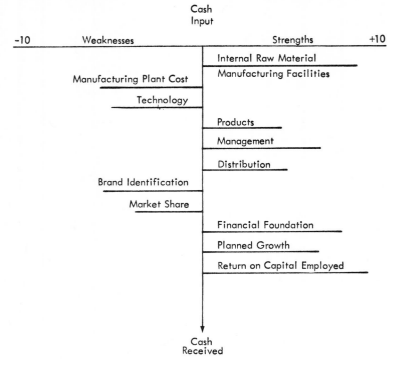

30 percent of the market, the relationship of profit to market share is suspect. Market share alone does not produce profitability. It does give well-managed firms another advantage which may lead to success.

Market share can be important when it is sufficiently high to have an influence on prices and sales. This can occur in products which have a declining life cycle, and a dominant influence can be achieved. In this situation, the advantage of the market share position would be short-lived as the product decayed in sales volume.

FINANCIAL STRUCTURE

A sound financial base will vary with time and economic conditions. An overly conservative balance sheet, one with excessive cash in relation to its basic capital requirements, could indicate a redundant management.

In such a situation, good management, innovative managers, and managers looking for a challenge will leave. Such companies, quite regularly, are acquired at bargain prices and turned into highly profitable operations. In these cases, the company and its employees survive in one form or another as part of a larger entity.

Such is not the case with the firm that is undercapitalized and is highly leveraged. On the downward side of the business cycle, many undercapitalized companies fail, particularly smaller ones. In the case of larger ones, there are substantial management changes. New capitalization with a heavy debt service cost is the penalty paid for fiscal mismanagement. This is usually the first step toward some form of bankruptcy in a highly competitive environment.

The 1960s was a time of fast growth. The availability of capital brought on by a period of unparalleled prosperity enabled nearly all segments of our society to accumulate money for investment. This reduced interest rates and made the formation of equity capital easy. It was a time to borrow, a time to fund through equity offerings despite marginal performance. In some cases, it was a basis to make cheap acquisition through share exchanges. These conditions led to excesses and to what amounted to nearly fraudulent offerings of equity stocks.

Excesses of this nature must come to an end. Generally, when the economy goes through such a cycle, there is a period of overcorrection. Thus, the mid-seventies have seen a scarcity of capital, a resistance by the investor to return to the market. With this comes high interest rates and a liquidity crisis. Managers need not look far to see who suffers in the "new" financial environment. It is the highly leveraged company. All too quickly the success story of one decade becomes the disaster of the next.

Such excesses need not happen in the well-managed company. It can maintain a balance, moving with conditions and capitalizing on the general economic cycle and its own industry cycle.

Some questions that should be asked are listed below.

1. What is the general working capital requirement in your industry?
2. How does the rest of the industry finance its working capital requirements?
3. Does your industry require a high ratio of working capital per dollar of fixed assets or is the reverse true?

The answers to each of these questions involve different financial structures.

As an example, assume that one competitor has financed his working capital requirements through an equity offering. Another firm may be using short-term loans or factoring. In this event, the firms using short-term loans and factoring will be at a competitive disadvantage to those firms which may have acquired cash through the sale of stock.

A company, for instance, which has a high working capital requirement per dollar of fixed assets should finance its business on short-term loans, particularly if it is subject to sharp changes in demand. To be burdened with a heavy debt in a highly cyclical business will inevitably lead to trouble. Similarly, a business which requires large amounts of capital for fixed asset placements (chemicals, petroleum, and fiber producers) will rely on long-term debt to finance its fixed asset requirements.

Where companies have large cash flow, normal debt requirements usually may be more easily handled; for the cash flow can support a large part of the company's working capital needs. As an example, for a bottling company profit as a percentage of sales may be quite low, but the cash flow as a percentage of sales is very attractive.

There are no hard and fast rules as to how a company should be structured. It is dependent upon a wide range of conditions within the particular industry, the age of the company, and the economy at a given point in time.

Sound management will establish certain basic requirements for its company. Managers will not deviate from these unless there is a unique series of happenings which result in change in the fiscal trends of an industry or in the economy that dictates a change. But, such changes happen very infrequently and are, therefore, the exception.

In the normal operation of a business, sound fiscal management has specific objectives in the area of capital structure which are unchanging. These objectives are to:

1. Get as much profitable growth as possible from the net worth of the company.
2. Build the company's investment credit so that additional capital is available for future expansion or to make attractive acquisitions in times of recession (the requirement for a sound credit rating is particularly important to relatively new or young companies).
3. Maintain a sound balance of assets so that capital employed does not get locked into excessive inventories, obsolete and inefficient plant or equipment.
4. Maintain a balanced equity and debt capital structure that permits growth equal to or better than industry growth without additional excessive cost.
5. Attain a capital position that circumvents or prevents a commitment to fixed costs that reduces the firm's flexibility and jeopardizes its position during a recession.

Management's attitude to these objectives and their success in dealing with them will determine, to a large extent, the short- and long-term success of the company.

There are no absolute rules that can dictate what proportion of various capital sources are the soundest for any given company at any given time. Generally, if it is possible, a relatively new company should rely on equity financing or new term money for its capital source.

Debt imposes fixed charges and tends to build fixed costs. It reduces a firm's ability to be flexible and to adjust to economic and industry conditions. In fact, the debt becomes the new firm's Achilles heel in times of intensive price competition and changes in the industry structure.

For the established company that is doing well, some debt can be taken on. Here too, it must be kept within workable limits. Normally, it should not exceed 40 percent of the total capital structure.

All too often, companies have undertaken debt to add plant and equipment without first analyzing the working capital needed to support the added volume resulting from the debt-financed expansion. Even inexpensive debt, such as local county industrial revenue bonds, should be closely scrutinized. Low cost industrial revenue bonds have caused many businesses to run aground.

Therefore, before new capital in any form is finalized and regardless of the "wisdom of management" for desiring the added funds, good management will pause and determine why it is needed. The total resources and the systems of the enterprise must be evaluated to determine if these are capable of supporting the added financial burden.

It is no longer enough in a world of rapid change, or shortages, to accept the old maxim of "growth financing." A much broader, more meaningful explanation is needed.

It has been known for a long time that new capital acquired for "financing growth" has really been taken on to mask poor management. Key questions involved are listed below.

1. Does the company have a good record of managing inventories or has it badly overinvested and mismanaged them over an extended period of time?
2. Is the cash flow adequate to maintain a possible excessive dividend rate?
3. Is the cash flow adequate to support the cost of servicing other debt forms as well?
4. Does the company have a history of adequate return on investment and a satisfactory cash flow in relation to capital employed?
5. Is the company in a high growth, average growth, or low growth industry?

If the answers to any of these questions are truly lacking, then the company is really using "growth financing" to overcome serious or potentially serious fiscal problems within the company.

CASH FORECASTING

A Cash Flow Statement for the year-ending financial results may be as indicated in Figure 10–4. This type of statement in some form is the basis of financial planning on a monthly, quarterly, or annual basis. A Typical Cash Forecast is displayed in Figure 10–5.

Once the forecast has been developed, the actual cash requirements can be compared with the forecast in a manner similar to a factory cost control statement (Chapter Five) showing standard, actual, and variance adjusted for sales volume. These need to be separated into fixed and variable cash so that management's attention can be concentrated on controllable financial components.

SHORT-TERM CASH MANAGEMENT

Short-term cash management includes a Daily Cash Report as indicated in Figure 10–6.

Such reports can be in more detail to include deposits by customer for accounts receivable and payments by supplier on accounts payable. With

FIGURE 10-4

Consolidated Source and Application of Funds Statement
(in thousands of dollars)

Year xxxx	
Sources of Funds	
Net earnings	50,000
Provision for depreciation and depletion	20,000
Deferral of income taxes	3,000
(Income)/loss absorbed on investments in other companies	3,000
Total funds from operations	$76,000
Issuance of common stock for acquired companies	1,000
Current maturity of state and municipal securities	4,000
Decrease in investments in other companies (net)	500
Net book value of property, plant and equipment sold	2,500
Proceeds from exercise of stock option	0
Increase in long term notes payable (net)	1,000
Other	0
Total funds provided	$85,000
Disposition of Funds	
Additions and improvements to property, plant, and equipment	$60,000
Additional investments in other companies (net)	5,000
Dividends	25,000
Purchase of common stock for treasury	0
Decrease in long-term notes payable (net)	0
Principal amount of debentures purchased for treasury	0
Other—decrease in working capital	(5,000)
Total funds expended	$85,000

computer applications, each customer who is within five days of paying a significant amount can be reported on an exception basis for follow-up by the Credit Department. Likewise, as the accounts receivable become past due, they can be analyzed daily for immediate attention.

Daily and hourly cash flow to include control of accounts receivable and accounts payable is an efficient application to real time data processing units. In this way, instantaneous cash maintenance can be provided throughout the entire firm, for all customers, suppliers, and cash needs. This enables constant monitoring of cash at various locations to expedite its movement into productive assets.

A schematic diagram of cash movement may be as indicated in Figure 10–7. Here, customer's bills are paid to regional sales offices with immediate deposits in local banks. Simultaneously, by the most efficient transmission method, the headquarter's office is notified. This permits immediate transfer from regional banks directly to a principal bank.

Wherever practical, delays in transmission of funds should be avoided.

FIGURE 10–5

Typical Cash Forecast

BUSINESS I
Cash Flow Forecast $000
For·Period xx/xx/xx through xx/xx/xx

	Sept.	Oct.	Nov.	Dec.	Jan.	Feb.	1st Quarter	2d Quarter	3d Quarter	4th Quarter
Beginning cash balance.	$ 25	$ 5	$ 25	$ 65	$ 30	$ 35	$ 70	$ 55	$ 20	$ 10
Cash Receipts:										
Sales.	110	115	110	115	125	130	400	420	435	490
Royalties.			20							20
Loans.						100	100			
Investment maturities.					40					
Others.	5	10	10	10	15	10	35	35	40	40
Total receipts:	115	125	140	125	180	240	535	455	475	550
Cash Disbursements:										
Accounts payable.	95	75	80	75	85	90	300	305	310	320
Payroll.	15	15	15	15	15	15	50	50	50	55
Taxes.	25	15	15	30	35	20	75	75	80	90
Loan repayments.					40		40		40	60
Dividends.							5			
Interest.							80		5	
Capital outlays.						80				
Investment purchases.				40				60		
Others.										
Total disbursements:	135	105	110	160	175	205	550	490	485	525
Ending cash balance.	$ 5	$ 25	$ 55	$ 35	$ 35	$ 70	$ 55	$ 20	$ 10	$ 35

FIGURE 10–6

Daily Cash Report

Date xx/xx/xx	
Bank balances at beginning of day	$ _____
Receipts:	
Deposits:	
Division A	$ _____
Division B	$ _____
Loans	$ _____
Other	$ _____
	$ _____
Disbursements:	
Accounts payable	$ _____
Payrolls	$ _____
Taxes	$ _____
Loan repayments	$ _____
Division A	$ _____
Division B	$ _____
Interest	$ _____
Capital expenditure payments	$ _____
Investments	$ _____
Other	$ _____
Bank balances at end of day	$ _____

Deposits can be directed to a principal bank rather than to a local one: transfers could be handled by the fastest available method. In some cases, couriers, even considering salary and expenses, can be efficient when large deposits are involved. Idle funds can be reduced by elimination of local banks, regional banks, or other delay points.

A key to quick deposit of accounts receivable is the form of payment by the customers. Some firms have centralized accounts receivable sections in large metropolitan areas, such as New York City or Chicago. These involve mail delays from throughout the country as well as at the metropolitan area. Cash payments can be expedited by setting up regional centers for collection. In many cases, these can be located in suburbs and away from mail bottlenecks.

CASH EFFICIENCY

Once an effective system has been developed to get cash into a regional or centralized bank, the financial manager must utilize the cash, either to reduce outstanding loans or to place it in interest-bearing accounts.

The key statistic is cash efficiency. This is defined as:

$$\text{Cash Efficiency} = \frac{\text{Total Cash Available} - \text{Idle Cash}}{\text{Total Cash Available}} \times 100$$

Idle cash is any money which has not been dispersed or utilized to obtain interest or income. This includes deposits which have not been transferred to income-earning accounts, advance payments of accounts payable, payments which have been accumulated but not deposited, or other inefficiencies.

A daily statistic of this type is invaluable to top management, as well as to the Financial Manager, to monitor the effectiveness of financial management. This is a guide to the proportion of cash which is working. It is similar to the efficiency on production equipment. However, it does not give a basis for determining the effectiveness of the cash utilized.

The yield on cash utilized is extremely important. "Are the funds being deposited in the most effective short-term instrument?" A guide to this is the accumulation of the interest or yield of surplus cash. This can be determined on a daily basis and annualized as a key statistic for management.

Continuous, daily, weekly, or other time interval cash management techniques have been well documented in other manuals and texts. A good one for review by the manager more interested in the mechanics of cash management is "Cash Management," The Conference Board, Report No. 580.

FIGURE 10–7

Schematic Diagram of Area Concentration Banking System

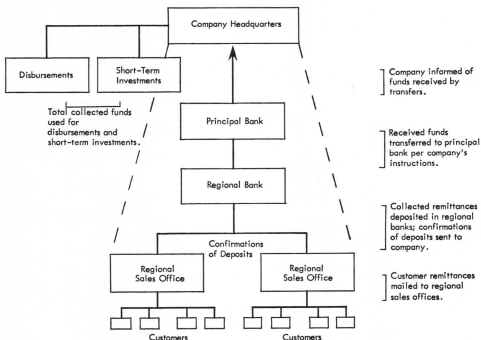

Improving the firm's cash position by nonpayment of accounts payable or by delaying payment is a matter of business integrity. Given acceptance of terms and contracts, the business manager has a responsibility to pay his accounts payable and suppliers within those terms. When terms are net 60 days, the supplier should have his payment in 60 days. To delay payment until the sixty-first day and then transmit it by slow mail is a questionable way to improve cash efficiency.

Breaking, or failing to meet, agreed upon terms with suppliers produces suspicion, sometimes unfounded. In some situations, the confidential disclosure of a short-term problem may be readily understood by suppliers from which unexpected help can be obtained.

FACTORING

With rapid growth in sales volume, it is difficult, even impossible, to finance growth from earnings. This necessitates the company's being satisfied with lower rates of growth or seeking outside methods of financing growth.

One method which permits inadequately financed businesses to grow rapidly has been factoring. In this situation, a bank commercial house takes over the credit function of the business, handles accounts receivable, and quickly returns cash to the business.

This is a useful method when properly controlled. Unfortunately, too many companies permit uncontrolled growth through factoring. As a result, the cash base will be stretched too far. Then, in a cyclical downturn, the company faces a liquidity crisis. Excessive interest is paid either to banks or financing groups. Many of these underfinanced companies fail.

Properly utilized, factoring can provide the basis for sales growth. Improperly utilized, factoring is an extremely dangerous financial tool.

LEASING

The leasing of equipment of all types (plant, office, and items of every other nature) is a way of generating funds for physical assets.

Leasing, in a limited way, can reduce the cash employed. Unfortunately, leasing reduces the depreciation and investment tax credits, and adversely affects cash flow.

As a result, those firms which are heavily involved in leased plant, property, and equipment have little or no cash flow in cyclical downturns or when profits deteriorate. This leaves the firms in a bad situation for cash. Many fail or become acquisition candidates.

For firms utilizing both factoring and leasing, the financial foundation very frequently is simply unable to absorb the shock of declining profits and high interest costs. As the financial base deteriorates, financial institutions increase interest rates which further penalizes the firm, causing a financial crisis. This causes the firm to cease to operate as a business and begin making decisions solely on cash demands.

Most conservative firms operate on a fully financed basis. Very few enterprises can function over the long term, fully financed.

Some outside financing is necessary and even desirable. Yet, when the interest load exceeds 1 percent to 2 percent of sales, the firm cannot recover this financial burden in the pricing of its products. Then, it becomes noncompetitive or profit margins are reduced.

The firms in the most difficult situation in a cyclical downturn are those which have excessive financing costs. It does not matter whether these are the result of excess plant, property, and equipment expansions, financing accounts receivable, leasing equipment, or other financial devices.

Over the short term, the successful firm has a sufficiently flexible financial base to permit it to retract and remain profitable in a downturn concurrent with the maintenance of sufficient cash to exploit desirable acquisitions when they occur. The manager who is constantly reacting within the constraints of heavy interest loads and creditors is not free to properly manage his business.

Historically, when a business begins to get into trouble, financial houses become involved either directly or indirectly in its management. This can cause incorrect decisions as few financial institution personnel are capable of making decisions and operating the business.

For a firm in a crisis which threatens its very survival, short- and long-term finances should be thoroughly evaluated. It may be that certain long-term loans should be converted to a short-term basis—even at a higher interest expense—to improve liquidity and short-term cash management.

Multi-national and holding companies sometimes create excessive interest costs in their subsidiaries. These parent companies tend to transfer profits of group companies to headquarters. This reduces the resources and forces the group companies to finance growth through external loans, rather than through their own cash flow. This can cause the group companies to face high financial costs and financial troubles.

Managers should:

Prepare an overlay of each business, each division, and each method of distribution to find the cash-hungry parts of the enterprise.

Separate capital into fixed and variable categories. Minimize the fixed portion to maintain profitability during a business slowdown.

Move the business into those areas where higher sales can be generated with less capital requirements—inventories, accounts receivable, and so forth.

Diagram cash requirements into strengths or weaknesses versus competition from cash input to cash received.

Prepare daily, weekly, monthly, or other time interval cash forecasts.

Study the movement of cash from receipt to utilization to eliminate delays or bottlenecks in transmission to interest earning or utilization.

Set up a "cash efficiency" control statistic on all funds, and avoid money stretching devices, such as factoring and leasing of equipment which will be a handicap.

Develop a financial plan so that interest and other financing expenses will not exceed 1 percent to 2 percent of sales.

Evaluate the total short- and long-term financial plan, and consider the possibility of converting some long-term financing to short-term requirements—even at a higher interest expense—to improve liquidity and short-term cash availability.

SUMMARY

The business of managers is money management. The one common foundation of successful business over the long term is sound financial management. Cash management is not the last chapter in this book because it is least important; it is last because it is most important!

First, the business must be viewed from a strategical point. This requires movement in plant and equipment or distribution to those areas which will generate the necessary sales per dollar of working capital and fixed assets. A diagram of cash requirements is displayed in this chapter. This and other visual diagrams are good ways to get perspectives on the total enterprise.

The importance of market share can be overemphasized. Although important in many cases, market share alone does not produce profitability.

In the "new" financial environment, the highly leveraged company may suffer. The success story of the past may be the disaster under the new conditions. Questions are asked to aid managers in developing a sound financial foundation.

Too often, companies undertake debt to add plant and equipment without first analyzing the working capital needed to support the added volume. There is a level of activity at which profits can be maximized. In general, this is the point where plant and equipment are fully utilized.

Cash forecasting and short-term cash management are discussed in these pages. Statements and forms for these purposes are displayed. Schematic diagrams of cash movements are a good way of finding where bottlenecks or delays can deteriorate cash utilization. Idle funds can be reduced by eliminating local banks, regional banks, or other delay points.

A key statistic is "cash efficiency." A daily statistic of this type is valuable to all managers to monitor the effectiveness of financial management. Managers should control the efficiency of cash in the same way production equipment is monitored.

Factoring and leasing of equipment can sometimes be helpful for financing purposes. However, too much interest on loans, too many leases of buildings and equipment, too much stretching of the available dollar (through factoring), and inadequate cash flow reduces the flexibility of the business to respond or cope with a business slowdown.

High or excessive interest expenses cannot be recovered in the market.

Although some outside financing is necessary or even desirable, the interest load for successful firms does not exceed 1 percent to 2 percent of sales.

The total financial plan of the firm should be evaluated. In the short term, it may be that certain long-term commitments should be converted to short-term financing—even at a higher interest expense. Short-term financing management for the firm in crisis involves expendable decisions which may require reversal in the long term.

The business of managers is cash management!

index

Index